Income tax rates (p. 1)

	2005–06	2004–05	2003–04
	%	%	%
Starting rate	10	10	10
Basic rate	22	22	22
Higher rate	40	40	40
Rate on non-dividend savings income	10/20/40[1]	10/20/40[1]	10/20/40[1]
Rate on dividend income	10/32.5[2]	10/32.5[2]	10/32.5[2]
Rate applicable to trusts	40	40	34
Schedule F trust rate	32.5	32.5	25
	£	£	£
Starting rate band	1–2,090	1–2,020	1–1,960
Basic rate band	2,091–32,400	2,021–31,400	1,961–30,500

Notes

[1] The rate of tax on non-dividend savings income is 10% for starting rate taxpayers, 20% for basic rate taxpayers, and 40% for higher rate taxpayers.

[2] The rate of tax on dividend income is 10%, and 32.5% at the higher rate.

Income tax reliefs (p. 4)

	2005–06 £	2004–05 £	2003–04 £	2002–03 £
Personal allowance	4,895	4,745	4,615	4,615
– age 65–74	7,090	6,830	6,610	6,100
– age 75 or over	7,220	6,950	6,720	6,370
Married couple's allowance[1]	–	–	–	–
– age less than 75 and born before				
6 April 1935	5,905	5,725	5,565	5,465
– age 75 or over	5,975	5,795	5,635	5,535
Maximum income before abatement				
of relief	19,500	18,900	18,300	17,900
Abatement income ceiling				
Single – age 65–74	23,890	23,070	22,290	20,870
– age 75 or over	24,150	23,310	22,510	21,410
Married – age 65–74	31,140	30,100	29,120	27,580
– age 75 or over	31,540	30,480	29,480	28,260
Blind person's allowance	1,610	1,560	1,510	1,480
'Rent-a-room' limit	4,250	4,250	4,250	4,250

Notes

[1] From 6 April 2000, the married couple's allowance, where both are under 65 years of age, and the additional allowance for children were withdrawn.

National Insurance contributions (p. 12)

Class 1 primary (employee) contributions	2005–06	2004–05
Lower earnings limit (LEL)	£82 weekly	£79 weekly
Primary threshold	£94 weekly	£91 weekly
Upper earnings limit (UEL)	£630 weekly	£610 weekly
Rate on earnings up to primary threshold	0%	0%
Not contracted-out rate	11% (£94.01–£630); 1% above £630	11% (£91.01–£610); 1% above £610
Contracted-out rate	9.4% (£94.01–£630); 1% above £630	9.4% (£91.01–£610); 1% above £610
Reduced rate	4.85% (£94.01–£630); 1% above £630	4.85% (£91.01–£610); 1% above £610

Class 1 secondary (employer) contributions 2005–06	
Secondary earnings threshold	£94 weekly £408 monthly £4,888 yearly
Not contracted-out rate	12.8% on earnings above threshold
Contracted-out rate	9.3% for salary-related (COSR) and 11.8% for money-purchase (COMP) schemes on earnings from secondary threshold to the UEL, then 12.8% on earnings above the UEL

Class 1 secondary (employer) contributions 2004–05	
Secondary earnings threshold	£91 weekly £395 monthly £4,732 yearly
Not contracted-out rate	12.8% on earnings above threshold
Contracted-out rate	9.3% for salary-related (COSR) and 11.8% for money-purchase (COMP) schemes on earnings from secondary threshold to the UEL, then 12.8% on earnings above the UEL

Class 2 – Self-employed	2005–06	2004–05	2003–04	2002–03
	£	£	£	£
Small earnings exemption limit (annual)	4,345	4,215	4,095	4,025
Weekly rate	2.10	2.05	2.00	2.00
Class 3 – Voluntary contributions	**2005–06**	**2004–05**	**2003–04**	**2002–03**
	£	£	£	£
Weekly rate	7.35	7.15	6.95	6.85
Class 4 – Self-employed	**2005–06**	**2004–05**	**2003–04**	**2002–03**
	£	£	£	£
Annual earnings limit – upper	32,760	31,720	30,940	30,420
– lower	4,895	4,745	4,615	4,615
Maximum contributions	–	–	–	1,806.35
Rate	8%	8%	8%	7%
	(£4,895–	(£4,745–	(£4,615–	
	£32,760);	£31,720);	£30,940);	
	1% above	1% above	1%	
	£32,760	£31,720	above	
			£30,940	

Taxation of capital gains (p. 58)

Exemptions and reliefs	2005–06	2004–05	2003–04	2002–03
	£	£	£	£
Annual exempt amount	8,500	8,200	7,900	7,700
Chattel exemption (max. sale proceeds)	6,000	6,000	6,000	6,000
Maximum retirement relief	—(1)	—(1)	—(1)	125,000

Note
(1) Retirement relief ceased to be available from 6 April 2003.

Inheritance tax (p. 74)

	Gross rate of tax	
Gross cumulative transfer (on or after 6 April 2005)	**Transfers on death**	**Lifetime transfers**
	%	%
£1–£275,000	Nil	Nil
£275,000 upwards	40	20

Note
Estate on death taxed as top slice of cumulative transfers in the seven years before death.
Most lifetime transfers (other than to discretionary trusts) are potentially exempt, only becoming chargeable where death occurs within seven years.

Annual exemption	£3,000
Small gift exemption	£250

Taxation of companies (p. 85)

Financial year	2005	2004	2003
Main rate	30%	30%	30%
Small companies' (SC) rate[1]	19%	19%	19%
Profit limit for SC rate	£300,000	£300,000	£300,000
Starting rate[1]	0%	0%	0%
Profit limit for starting rate	£10,000	£10,000	£10,000
Profit limit for starting rate marginal relief	£50,000	£50,000	£50,000
Marginal relief fraction (starting rate)	19/400	19/400	19/400
Marginal relief fraction (SC rate)	11/400	11/400	11/400

Note
[1] The starting rate and small companies' rate are not available to 'close investment-holding companies'.

VAT (p. 155)

Standard rate	17.5%
Annual registration limit – taxable supplies (from 1 April 2005)	£60,000
De-registration limit – taxable supplies (from 1 April 2005)	£58,000
VAT fraction	7/47

PREFACE

Now in its 24th edition, *Hardman's Tax Rates & Tables* contains the numerical and factual data in everyday use by the tax practitioner. The material is conveniently arranged in fifteen sections:

- Principles of income tax
- Tax credits
- National Insurance contributions
- Taxation of business profits
- Taxation of investment income
- Taxation of earnings
- Taxation of capital gains
- Inheritance tax
- Taxation of companies
- General
- Stamp taxes
- Value added tax
- Insurance premium tax
- Landfill tax
- Aggregates levy

The book contains the latest available data at the time of going to press. It takes full account of the *Finance Act 2005*. Foreign exchange rates to December 2004 and April 2005 are published later in the year. These will be included in the second edition to be published in December.

Every effort has been taken to include, within the constraints of available space, the information of greatest use to the practitioner. A number of changes have been made in the light of suggestions received from users of previous years' editions. CCH welcomes further suggestions as to material which might be inserted in future editions.

May 2005

Note: the late Philip Hardman was the original editor of Hardman's Tax Rates & Tables. CCH gratefully acknowledges the considerable help and guidance that he provided.

Disclaimer

This publication is sold on the understanding that the publisher is not engaged in rendering legal or accounting advice or other professional services. The publisher, its editors and any authors, consultants or general editors expressly disclaim all and any liability and responsibility to any person, whether purchaser or reader of this publication or not, in respect of anything and of the consequences of anything, done or omitted to be done by any such person in reliance, whether wholly or partially, upon the whole or any part of the contents of this publication. While this publication is intended to provide accurate information in regard to the subject matter covered, readers entering into transactions on the basis of such information should seek the services of a competent professional adviser.

Legislative and other material

While copyright in all statutory and other materials resides in the Crown or other relevant body, copyright in the remaining material in this publication is vested in the publisher.

The publisher advises that any statutory or other materials issued by the Crown or other relevant bodies and reproduced and quoted in this publication are not the authorized official versions of those statutory or other materials. In the preparation, however, the greatest care has been taken to ensure exact conformity with the law as enacted or other material as issued.

Crown copyright legislation is reproduced under the terms of Crown Copyright Policy Guidance issued by HMSO. Other Crown copyright material is reproduced with the permission of the controller of HMSO. European Communities Copyright material is reproduced with permission.

ISBN 1 84140 649 X
CCH Code 5010A

© 2005 Wolters Kluwer (UK) Ltd

Printed and bound in Great Britain by Clays Ltd, St Ives plc.

About the Publisher

CCH is part of the Wolters Kluwer Group. Wolters Kluwer is the leading international publisher specialising in tax, business and law publishing throughout Europe, the US and the Asia Pacific region. The Group produces a wide range of information services in different media for the accounting and legal professions and for business.

All CCH publications are designed to be practical and authoritative reference works and guides and are written by our own highly qualified and experienced editorial team and specialist outside authors.

CCH publishes information packages including electronic products, loose-leaf reporting services, newsletters and books on UK and European legal topics for distribution world-wide. The UK operation also acts as distributor of the publications of the overseas affiliates.

CCH
145 London Road
Kingston-upon-Thames
Surrey
KT2 6SR
Telephone: 0870 777 2906
Facsimile: 0208 247 1184
email: customerservices@cch.co.uk
website: www.cch.co.uk

Part of the Wolters Kluwer Group

Acknowledgements

Certain material in this publication is Crown Copyright and is reproduced with the kind permission of the Controller of Her Majesty's Stationery Office.

CCH kindly acknowledges the endorsement of this publication by the Chartered Institute of Taxation and the Tax Faculty of the Institute of Chartered Accountants in England and Wales.

THE CHARTERED INSTITUTE OF TAXATION

PRINCIPLES OF INCOME TAX

Income tax rates

2005–06

	Taxable income band £	Tax rate %	Tax on band £
Starting rate	0– 2,090	10	209.00
Basic rate	2,091–32,400	22	6,668.20
Higher rate	Over 32,400	40	

Rate on non-dividend savings income	10% up to starting rate limit 20% up to basic rate limit 40% thereafter
Rate on dividend income	10% up to basic rate limit 32.5% thereafter
Rate applicable to trusts	40%
Schedule F trust rate	32.5%

2004–05

	Taxable income band £	Tax rate %	Tax on band £
Starting rate	0– 2,020	10	202.00
Basic rate	2,021–31,400	22	6,463.60
Higher rate	Over 31,400	40	

Rate on non-dividend savings income	10% up to starting rate limit 20% up to basic rate limit 40% thereafter
Rate on dividend income	10% up to basic rate limit 32.5% thereafter
Rate applicable to trusts	40%
Schedule F trust rate	32.5%

2

2003–04

	Taxable income band £	Tax rate %	Tax on band £
Starting rate	0– 1,960	10	196.00
Basic rate	1,961–30,500	22	6,278.80
Higher rate	Over 30,500	40	

Rate on non-dividend savings income	10% up to starting rate limit 20% up to basic rate limit 40% thereafter
Rate on dividend income	10% up to basic rate limit 32.5% thereafter
Rate applicable to trusts	34%
Schedule F trust rate	25%

2002–03

	Taxable income band £	Tax rate %	Tax on band £
Starting rate	0– 1,920	10	192.00
Basic rate	1,921–29,900	22	6,155.60
Higher rate	Over 29,900	40	

Rate on non-dividend savings income	10% up to starting rate limit 20% up to basic rate limit 40% thereafter
Rate on dividend income	10% up to basic rate limit 32.5% thereafter
Rate applicable to trusts	34%
Schedule F trust rate	25%

2001–02

	Taxable income band £	Tax rate %	Tax on band £
Starting rate	0– 1,880	10	188.00
Basic rate	1,881–29,400	22	6,054.40
Higher rate	Over 29,400	40	

Rate on non-dividend savings income	10% up to starting rate limit 20% up to basic rate limit 40% thereafter
Rate on dividend income	10% up to basic rate limit 32.5% thereafter
Rate applicable to trusts	34%
Schedule F trust rate	25%

2000–01

	Taxable income band £	Tax rate %	Tax on band £
Starting rate	0– 1,520	10	152.00
Basic rate	1,521–28,400	22	5,913.60
Higher rate	Over 28,400	40	

Rate on non-dividend savings income	10% up to starting rate limit 20% up to basic rate limit 40% thereafter
Rate on dividend income	10% up to basic rate limit 32.5% thereafter
Rate applicable to trusts	34%
Schedule F trust rate	25%

1999–2000

	Taxable income band £	Tax rate %	Tax on band £
Starting rate	0– 1,500	10	150.00
Basic rate	1,501–28,000	23	6,095.00
Higher rate	Over 28,000	40	

Rate on non-dividend savings income	10% up to starting rate limit 20% up to basic rate limit 40% thereafter
Rate on dividend income	10% up to basic rate limit 32.5% thereafter
Rate applicable to trusts	34%
Schedule F trust rate	25%

Personal allowances and reliefs

Type of relief	2005–06 £	2004–05 £	2003–04 £	2002–03 £	2001–02 £	2000–01 £	1999–00 £
Personal allowance							
Age under 65	4,895	4,745	4,615	4,615	4,535	4,385	4,335
Age 65–74	7,090	6,830	6,610	6,100	5,990	5,790	5,720
Age 75 & over	7,220	6,950	6,720	6,370	6,260	6,050	5,980
Married couple's allowance[1]							
Born after 6 April 1935	–	–	–	–	–	–	1,970
Born before 6 April 1935;							
Age up to 74	5,905	5,725	5,565	5,465	5,365	5,185	5,125
Born before 6 April 1935;							
Age 75 & over	5,975	5,795	5,635	5,535	5,435	5,255	5,195
Minimum amount of allowance	2,280	2,210	2,150	2,110	2,070	2,000	–
Maximum income before abatement of reliefs for older taxpayers:	19,500	18,900	18,300	17,900	17,600	17,000	16,800
Abatement income ceiling							
Personal allowance:							
Age 65–74	23,890	23,070	22,290	20,870	20,510	19,810	19,570
Age 75 & over	24,150	23,310	22,510	21,410	21,050	20,330	20,090
Married couples allowance							
Born before 6 April 1935;							
Age up to 74	31,140	30,100	29,120	27,580	27,100	26,180	25,880
Born before 6 April 1935;							
Age 75 & over	31,540	30,480	29,480	28,260	27,780	26,840	26,540

Type of relief	2005–06 £	2004–05 £	2003–04 £	2002–03 £	2001–02 £	2000–01 £	1999–00 £
Additional allowance for children	–	–	–	–	–	–	1,970
Children's tax credit[2] Baby rate	–	–	–	5,290 10,490	5,200	–	–
Widow's bereavement allowance	–	–	–	–	–	–	1,970
Blind person's allowance	1,610	1,560	1,510	1,480	1,450	1,400	1,380
Life assurance relief (policies issued before 14 March 1984)	12.5% of premiums	12.5% of premiums	12.5% of premiums	12.5% of premiums	12.5% of premiums	12.5% of premiums	12.5% of premiums
Mortgage interest Loan limit	–	–	–	–	–	–	30,000
'Rent-a-room' limit	4,250	4,250	4,250	4,250	4,250	4,250	4,250

Notes
[1] From 1999–2000 onwards relief is given at a rate of 10%.
[2] Children's Tax Credit was given at the rate of 10% and withdrawn by £2 for every £3 by which the claimant's income exceeded the higher rate threshold.

Submission dates for 2005–06 personal tax returns

The return must be filed by 31 January 2007, except in the following circumstances:

Circumstances	Filing date
Taxpayer wishes the Revenue to calculaté the tax liability in time for the first payment date or repayment: • return issued by 31 July 2006	30 September 2006 (paper returns); 31 December 2006 (electronically delivered returns)
• return issued after 31 July 2006	Two months from date of issue
Taxpayer making self-assessment – return issued after 31 October 2006	Three months from date of issue
Taxpayer wishes underpayment (below £2,000) to be coded out under 2007-08 PAYE (paper returns)	30 September 2006
Taxpayer wishes underpayment (below £2,000) to be coded out under 2007-08 PAYE (electronically delivered returns)	31 December 2006

6

Main penalty provisions

Individuals: 2005–06

Offence	Penalty[1][2]
Late return (TMA 1970, s. 93)[3][4]: • if return not filed by 1 February 2007 • if return still not filed by 31 July 2007 • if return not filed after 1 February 2008 • for continuing delay on application to the commissioners	£100 £100 Tax geared Up to £60 per day
Failure to notify chargeability (TMA 1970, s. 7)	Tax geared
Incorrect return, accounts and claims made fraudulently or negligently (TMA 1970, s. 95)	Tax geared
Failure to keep and retain tax records (TMA 1970, s. 12B)	Up to £3,000 per year of assessment
False statements to reduce interim payments (TMA 1970, s. 59A)	Tax geared
Failure to produce documents in an enquiry (TMA 1970, s. 97AA): • initial penalty • daily penalty	 £50 £30/£150[5]

Notes

[1] Interest is charged on penalties not paid when due. The due date is 30 days after the notice of determination of the penalty is issued.

[2] A defence of 'reasonable excuse' may be available.

[3] Late return penalties are cumulative, e.g. for a return six or more months late there are two £100 penalties.

[4] The two fixed £100 penalties are reduced if the total tax payable by assessment is less than the penalty which would otherwise be chargeable.

[5] The lower daily rate applies when determination of the penalty was made by the inspector, the higher when determination was made by the commissioners.

Partnerships: 2005–06

Offence	Penalty[1][2]
Late return (TMA 1970, s. 93A)[3][4]: • if return not filed by 1 February 2007 • if return not filed by 31 July 2007 • for continuing delay on application to the commissioners	£100 £100 Up to £60 per day

Offence	Penalty[1][2]
Failure to notify chargeability	None (but individual partners face a tax-geared penalty under TMA 1970, s. 7)
Incorrect return, accounts and claims made fraudulently or negligently (TMA 1970, s. 95A)	Tax geared
Failure to keep and retain tax records (TMA 1970, s. 12B)	Up to £3,000 per year of assessment
Failure to produce documents in enquiry (TMA 1970, s. 97AA): • initial penalty • daily penalty	 £50 £30/£150[5]

Notes

[1] Interest is charged on penalties not paid when due. The due date is 30 days after the notice of determination of the penalty is issued.

[2] A defence of 'reasonable excuse' on the part of the representative partner or his successor may be available.

[3] Late return penalties are cumulative, e.g. for a return six or more months late there are two £100 penalties.

[4] Late return penalties apply to each partner (e.g. short delay = £100 per partner).

[5] The lower daily rate applies when determination of the penalty was made by the inspector, the higher when determination was made by the commissioners.

TAX CREDITS

Working tax credits and child tax credits

Working tax credit – maximum rates 2003–04 to 2005–06

Element	2003–04 £	2004–05 £	2005–06 £
Basic element	1,525	1,570	1,620
Disability element (see note below)	2,040	2,100	2,165
30-hour element	620	640	660
Second adult element	1,500	1,545	1,595
Lone parent element	1,500	1,545	1,595
50-plus element; (a) working over 16 but less than 30 hours per week	1,045	1,075	1,110
(b) working over 30 hours per week (see note below)	1,565	1,610	1,660
Childcare element: 70% of eligible costs up to a weekly maximum of: • for one child	£135		£170
• for two or more	£200		£300

Child tax credit – maximum rates 2003–04 to 2005–06

Element	Circumstance	Maximum annual rate 2003–04 £	Maximum annual rate 2004–05 £	Maximum annual rate 2005–06 £
Family	Normal case	545	545	545
	Where there is a child under the age of one	1,090	1,090	1,090
Individual	Each child or young person	1,455	1,625	1,690
	Each disabled child or young person	3,600	3,840	3,975
	Each severely disabled child or young person	4,465	4,730	4,895

Income thresholds and withdrawal rates 2003–04 to 2005–06

	2003–04	2004–05	2005–06
First income threshold	£5,060	£5,060	£5,220
First withdrawal rate	37%	37%	37%
Second income threshold	£50,000	£50,000	£50,000
Second withdrawal rate	6.67%	6.67%	6.67%
First threshold for those entitled to Child Tax Credit only	£13,480	£13,480	£13,910
Income disregard	£2,500	£2,500	£2,500

Working families' tax credit

Working families' tax credit (WFTC)[1][4]

Amounts shown in £'s per week

		2002–03	2001–02
Basic tax credit		62.50 (before 4 June 2002, 60.00)	59.00 (before 4 June 2001, 54.00)
Credit where one earner worked at least 30 hours per week		11.65	11.45
Child tax credits	Up to 16	26.45	26.00
	16–18	27.20	26.75
	Disabled child	35.50	30.00
Enhanced disability tax credit[2]	lone parent/ couple	16.25	16.00
	child	11.25	11.05
Maximum income before taper[3]		94.50	92.90

Notes

[1] The WFTC was available to claimants who were in work, who were responsible for a child or young person, whose net household income did not exceed a prescribed limit, and whose savings did not exceed £8,000. WFTC was administered by the Revenue and was paid to employed claimants via their employer. Self-employed people received WFTC direct from the Revenue. Couples were able to choose whether the mother or father received the WFTC. The WFTC award was calculated by adding the credits together and will normally last for 26 weeks.

[2] The enhanced disability tax credit was available for people who were in receipt of the highest rate care component of disability living allowance.

[3] The WFTC was withdrawn at the rate of 55p in every £1 by which net household income exceeded the weekly threshold shown.
[4] The WFTC was replaced by the working tax credit and child tax credit for 2003-04 onwards.

Disabled person's tax credit

Disabled person's tax credit (DPTC)[1][4]

Amounts shown in £'s per week

		2002–03	2001–02
Basic tax credit	Single person	62.10	61.05 (before 4 June 2001, 56.05)
	Couple or lone parent	95.30 (before 4 June 2002, 92.80)	91.25 (before 4 June 2001, 86.25)
Credit where claimant or partner worked at least 30 hours per week		11.65	11.45
Child tax credits	Up to 16	26.45	26.00
	16–18	27.20	26.75
	Disabled child	35.50	30.00
Enhanced disability tax credit[2]	Single person	11.25	11.05
	lone parent/ couple	16.25	16.00
	child	11.25	11.05
Maximum income before taper[3]	Single person	73.50	72.25
	Couple or lone parent	94.50	92.90

Notes
[1] The DPTC was payable to a claimant with an illness or disability that put him or her at a disadvantage in getting a job, who received one of a number of qualifying benefits, whose net household income did not exceed a prescribed

amount, and whose savings did not exceed £16,000. It was administered by the Revenue and was paid to employed claimants via their employer.

[2] The enhanced disability tax credit was available to people who were in receipt of the highest rate care component of disability living allowance.

[3] The DPTC was withdrawn by 55p for every £1 by which net household income exceeded the weekly thresholds shown.

[4] The DPTC was replaced by the working tax credit and child tax credit for 2003-04 onwards

Childcare tax credit

	2002–03	2001–02
Childcare tax credit	70% of eligible childcare costs up to a maximum of: • £135 a week costs for one child (i.e. maximum of £94.50 credit); and • £200 a week costs for more than one (i.e. maximum of £140 credit).	70% of eligible childcare costs up to a maximum of: **Pre June 2001:** • £100 a week costs for one child (i.e. maximum of £70 credit); and • £150 a week for more than one (i.e. maximum of £105 credit). **From June 2001:** • £135 a week costs for one child (i.e. maximum of £94.50 credit); and • £200 a week costs for more than one (i.e. maximum £140 credit).

NATIONAL INSURANCE CONTRIBUTIONS

NIC rates: general

There are five classes of National Insurance contributions payable according to the individual circumstances of the payer.

Class 1 contributions

Class 1 contributions are earnings related. An employee and his employer must pay such contributions if his earnings reach the primary threshold. Employees' contributions are paid on all earnings above the primary threshold and below the upper limit.

The reduced rate applies to married women or widows with a valid certificate of election. Men over 65 and women over 60 pay no primary contributions, though employers still pay the secondary contribution, usually at the non-contracted out rate, regardless of the previous category of contribution liability. Children under 16 and their employers pay no contributions.

Class 1 NIC: 2005–06

Class 1 contributions

Class 1 primary (employee) contributions 2005–06	
Lower earnings limit (LEL)[1]	£82 weekly £356 monthly £4,264 yearly
Primary threshold	£94 weekly £408 monthly £4,888 yearly
Upper earnings limit (UEL)	£630 weekly £2,730 monthly £32,760 yearly
Rate on earnings up to primary threshold	0%
Not contracted-out rate	11% on £94.01 to £630 weekly 1% on excess over £630
Contracted-out rate	9.4% on £94.01 to £630 weekly 1% on excess over £630
Reduced rate[2]	4.85% on £94.01 to £630 weekly 1% on excess over £630

Notes

(1) Earnings from the LEL, up to and including the primary threshold will count towards the employee's basic 'flat rate' state pension, even though no contributions will have been paid on those earnings. Similarly, earnings between the lower earnings limit (LEL) and the primary threshold will count towards the employee's entitlement to certain benefits including the additional pension (SERPS) or, from April 2002, the second state pension.

(2) The reduced rate applies to married women or widows with a valid certificate of election. Men over 65 and women over 60 pay no primary contributions, though employers still pay the secondary contribution at the usual rate. People under 16 and their employers pay no contributions.

Class 1 secondary (employer) contributions 2005–06(1)	
Earnings threshold	£94 weekly £408 monthly £4,888 yearly
Not contracted-out rate	12.8% above earnings threshold
Contracted-out rate(2)(3)	9.3% for salary-related (COSR) and 11.8% for money-purchase (COMP) schemes (including 3.5% and 1.0% rebates for earnings from LEL to secondary threshold), then 12.8% above UEL.

Notes

(1) Class 1 contributions are earnings related. Employees must pay primary Class 1 contributions on that part of their earnings which exceeds the primary threshold, up to the upper earnings limit.

(2) Earnings from the LEL, up to and including the primary threshold will count towards the employee's basic 'flat rate' state pension, even though no contributions will have been paid on those earnings. Similarly, earnings between the lower earnings limit (LEL) and the primary threshold will count towards the employee's entitlement to certain benefits including the additional pension (SERPS) or, from April 2002, the second state pension.

(3) With contracted-out salary related (COSR) schemes there is an employer's NIC rebate of 3.5 per cent of earnings above the employer's earnings threshold, up to and including the upper earnings limit. With contracted-out money purchase (COMP) schemes there is an employer's NIC rebate of 1 per cent of earnings above the employer's earnings threshold, up to and including the upper earnings limit and a further age-related rebate is paid by the Inland Revenue National Insurance Contributions Office directly into the scheme.

Class 1 NIC: 2004–05

Class 1 contributions

Class 1 primary (employee) contributions 2004–05	
Lower earnings limit (LEL)(1)	£79 weekly £343 monthly £4,108 yearly
Primary threshold	£91 weekly £395 monthly £4,745 yearly

Class 1 primary (employee) contributions 2004–05	
Upper earnings limit (UEL)	£610 weekly £2,644 monthly £31,720 yearly
Rate on earnings up to primary threshold	0%
Not contracted-out rate	11% on £91.01 to £610 weekly 1% on excess over £610
Contracted-out rate	9.4% on £91.01 to £610 weekly 1% on excess over £610
Reduced rate[2]	4.85% on £91.01 to £610 weekly 1% excess over £610

Notes

[1] Earnings from the LEL, up to and including the primary threshold will count towards the employee's basic 'flat rate' state pension, even though no contributions will have been paid on those earnings. Similarly, earnings between the lower earnings limit (LEL) and the primary threshold will count towards the employee's entitlement to certain benefits including the additional pension (SERPS) or, from April 2002, the second state pension.

[2] The reduced rate applies to married women or widows with a valid certificate of election. Men over 65 and women over 60 pay no primary contributions, though employers still pay the secondary contribution at the usual rate. People under 16 and their employers pay no contributions.

Class 1 secondary (employer) contributions 2004–05	
Secondary earnings threshold	£91 weekly £395 monthly £4,745 yearly
Not contracted-out rate	12.8% on earnings above threshold
Contracted-out rate	9.3% for salary-related (COSR) and 11.8% for money-purchase (COMP) schemes on earnings from secondary threshold to the UEL, then 12.8% on earnings above the UEL

Class 1A contributions

From 6 April 2000, employers (but not employees) pay NICs on an annual basis on benefits in kind provided to employees earning at the rate of £8,500 p.a. or more or to directors. The Class 1A rate for 2004–05 and 2005–06 is 12.8 per cent. Contributions for the year are due by 19 July following the end of the tax year to which they relate.

Prior to 6 April 2000, employers (but not employees) paid NICs on an annual basis on cars or fuel provided for the private use of employees earning at the rate of £8,500 p.a. or more or for directors. The liability is calculated on the income tax car and fuel scale rates.

Return deadlines for Class 1 and 1A contributions

Forms	Date	Penalty provision
End of year returns P14, P35, P38 and P38A	19 May following year of assessment	TMA 1970, s. 98A
P11D(b)	6 July following year of assessment	SI 2001/1004, reg. 81(2)

Note

In cases of PAYE and NIC default there are provisions to prevent double charging. Class 1A contributions are recorded annually in arrears. Penalties will only be imposed if there is a delay in the submission of the relevant year's PAYE return.

Class 1B contributions

Rate of Class 1B contributions

From 6 April 1999 Class 1B contributions are payable by employers on the amount of emoluments in a PAYE settlement agreement (PSA) which are chargeable to Class 1 or Class 1A NICs, together with the total amount of income tax payable under the agreement. Class 1B contributions are charged at a rate equal to the secondary rate of NICs with power for the Secretary of State to alter the rate by statutory instrument; but not so as to increase it to more than two per cent above the rate applicable at the end of the preceding year.

Class 2 contributions

Class 2 contributions

Class 2 contributions are paid at a flat rate by a self-employed person unless he has applied for and been granted exception because his earnings are below the exception (SEE) limit for Class 2 contributions. If a person is excepted, he may still pay the contributions voluntarily to keep up his right to the benefits they provide.

Rates and SEE limit

	Weekly contribution rate			
Tax year	Rate £	Share fishermen £	Volunteer development workers £	Small earnings exceptional limit £
2005–06	2.10	2.75	4.10	4,345
2004–05	2.05	2.70	3.95	4,215
2003–04	2.00	2.65	3.85	4,095

| Tax year | Weekly contribution rate | | | Small earnings exceptional limit £ |
	Rate £	Share fishermen £	Volunteer development workers £	
2002–03	2.00	2.65	3.75	4,025
2001–02	2.00	2.65	3.60	3,955
2000–01	2.00	2.65	3.35	3,825
1999–00	6.55	7.20	3.30	3,770

Class 3 contributions

Class 3 contributions

Class 3 contributions are paid voluntarily by persons not liable for contributions, or who have been excepted from Class 2 contributions, or whose contribution record is insufficient to qualify for benefits. They are paid at a flat rate.

Rate and earnings factor

Tax year	Weekly contribution rate £	Earnings factor for each contribution in col. 2 £
2005–06	7.35	82.00
2004–05	7.15	79.00
2003–04	6.95	77.00
2002–03	6.85	75.00
2001–02	6.75	72.00
2000–01	6.55	67.00
1999–00	6.45	66.00

Class 4 contributions

Class 4 contributions

Self-employed people whose profits or gains are over a certain amount have to pay Class 4 contributions as well as Class 2 contributions. These contributions are earnings related and paid at a higher rate on earnings between the lower and upper earnings limits and at one per cent thereafter.

Tax year	Rate on profits between upper and lower limits %	Annual lower profits limit £	Annual upper profits limit £	Rate on profits in excess of upper limit %	Maximum contribution £
2005–06	8	4,895	32,760	1	unlimited
2004–05	8	4,745	31,720	1	unlimited
2003–04	8	4,615	30,940	1	unlimited
2002–03	7	4,615	30,420	0	1,806.35
2001–02	7	4,535	29,900	0	1,775.55
2000–01	7	4,385	27,820	0	1,640.45
1999–00	6	7,530	26,000	0	1,108.20

Annual maximum contributions for years up to 2002–03

Following the introduction of additional primary Class 1 contributions on earnings above the upper earnings limit from 6 April 2003, the annual maximum applicable to each individual will vary according to their earnings. It is therefore no longer possible to calculate a single figure which will be of universal application.

For the limit placed on a person's total NIC liability under Class 1, Class 2 and Class 4, see the centre column of the table below.

Where a person's total Class 1 and Class 2 contributions in a tax year are less than the figure given in the second column in the table, his Class 4 liability is limited to the difference between that total and the figure in the third column.

Tax year	Overall maximum £	Class 4 maximum £
2002–03	2,628.80	1,912.35
2001–02	2,586.40	1,881.55
2000–01	2,432.70	1,746.45
1999–00	2,300.20	1,455.35

TAXATION OF BUSINESS PROFITS

Farming and market gardening: relief for fluctuating profits
(ITTOIA 2005, S 221–225)

Full averaging (ITTOIA 2005, s. 223(3))
Full averaging pplies where profits for either relevant tax year do not exceed 70 per cent of profits for the other year or are nil.

Marginal averaging (ITTOIA 2005, s. 223(4))
The amount of the adjustment to the profits of each relevant tax year, where lower profits are between 70 and 75 per cent of higher profits, is computed as follows::

$$3 \, ((75\% \ H) - L)$$

where

H   is the higher profit; and

L   is the lower profit.

Creative artists: relief for fluctuating profits
(ITTOIA 2005, s. 221)

Full averaging (ITTOIA 2005, s. 223(3))
As with farming and market gardening, full averaging applies where profits for either relevant tax year do not exceed 70 per cent of profits for the other year or are nil.

Marginal averaging (ITTOIA 2005, s. 223(4))
As with farming and market gardening, the amount of the adjustment to the profits of each relevant tax year, where lower profits are between 70 and 75 per cent of higher profits, is computed as follows:

$$3 \, ((75\% \ H) - L)$$

where

H   is the higher profit; and

L   is the lower profit.

Time limits for elections and claims
In the absence of any provision to the contrary, under self-assessment for the purposes of income tax, the normal rule is that claims are to be made within five years from 31 January next following the tax year to which they relate (TMA 1970, s. 43(1)).

In certain cases the Board *may* permit an extension of the strict time limit in relation to certain elections and claims.

Provision	Time limit	Statutory reference
Averaging of profits of farmers or creative artists	12 months from 31 January next following end of the second tax year concerned	ITTOIA 2005, s. 222
Stock transferred to a connected party on cessation of trade to be valued at higher cost or sale price	2 years from end of accounting period in which trade ceased	ITTOIA 2005, s. 175
Post-cessation expenses relieved against income and chargeable gains	12 months from 31 January next following the tax year	ITTOIA 2005, s. 257(4)
Current and preceding year set-off of trading losses	12 months from 31 January next following the tax year loss arose	ICTA 1988, s. 380; FA 1991, s.72
Three-year carry-back of trading losses in opening years of trade	12 months from 31 January next following the tax year loss arose	ICTA 1988, s. 381(1)
Carry-forward of trading losses	5 years from 31 January next following tax year in which loss arose	ICTA 1988, s. 385(1)
Carry-back of terminal losses	5 years from 31 January next following tax year	ICTA 1988, s. 388(1)
Certain plant and machinery treated as 'short life' assets (income tax elections)	12 months from 31 January next following the tax year in which ends the chargeable period in which the qualifying expenditure was incurred	CAA 2001, s. 85
Transfer between connected parties of certain assets, eligible for capital allowances, at tax-written down value	2 years from date of sale	CAA 2001, s. 570(5)

TAXATION OF INVESTMENT INCOME

Personal pension contributions (PPCs) and retirement annuity premiums (RAPs)

From 6 April 2001, pension providers are able to offer stakeholder pensions. The tax regime for personal pensions has been adapted to fit the regime applying to stakeholder pensions.

From 2001–02, contributions can be made to personal schemes *from any source* (not necessarily earnings) up to the level of the 'earnings threshold' for the year. The earnings threshold is a gross figure – the contributor makes a net contribution and the government tops it up by the basic rate of tax, whether or not the payment has been made out of taxed income.

Tax year	Earnings threshold (gross) – £	Earnings threshold (net) – £
From 2001–02	3,600	2,808

From 2001–02, contributions to personal pensions in excess of the earnings threshold may be made out of *earned income only* to the extent of the age-related percentage of the contributor's net relevant earnings for the year, up to the earnings cap – see tables below. Tax relief on higher rate contributions is recoverable through self-assessment.

Retirement annuities are unaffected by the 2001 changes in personal pensions.

Tax year	Age of taxpayer (at the beginning of the tax year) (ICTA 1988, s. 626, 640(2))	Limit of allowable payment	
		PPCs %	RAPs %
1989–90 to 2005–06 inclusive	35 or less	17.5	17.5
	36–45	20	17.5
	46–50	25	17.5
	51–55	30	20
	56–60	35	22.5
	61–75	40	27.5

RAPS: Carry-forward of relief: in calculating the maximum relief deductible in a year, the relief (not premiums/contributions paid) which was not used in an earlier year can be carried forward and used in any of the following six years (ICTA 1988, s. 625, 642). Relief which is carried forward is used on a first-in, first-out basis. This is abolished in respect of PPCs for 2001–02 and subsequent years.

PPCs: nominating a 'basis year': Where net relevant earnings exceed the earnings threshold, PPCs in 2001–02 and later years may be based on net relevant earnings in any one of the previous five years (ICTA 1988, s. 646B, 646C). Such 'higher level contributions' may also be made for five years after a year in which earnings have ceased.

Carry-back of contributions or premiums: PPCs paid in 2001–02 or any later tax year may be treated as paid in the previous tax year, provided that the contribution is paid on or before 31 January in the later year, and the payer makes an irrevocable election on or before the date of payment. For retirement annuity premiums, and personal pension contributions in 2000–01 and earlier years, an individual can elect to treat all or part of a payment made in one year as if it was paid in the last preceding year, or if he had *no* 'net relevant earnings' in that last preceding year then he can elect to treat it as paid in the last preceding year but one (ICTA 1988, s. 619(4), 641(1); Form 43, PP42 and PP43 in respect of retirement annuity premiums and personal pension contributions respectively).

Where an individual pays both PPCs and RAPs maximum allowable PPCs (computed by reference to the earnings cap or otherwise) are reduced by qualifying RAPs paid and given relief in the tax year (ICTA 1988, s. 655(1)).

The 'Earnings cap': personal pension contributions (PPCs) 'allowable maximum' (ICTA 1988, s. 640A, 646A) and employers' Retirement Benefit Schemes 'permitted maximum' remuneration (ICTA 1988, s. 509C)

Tax year	Maximum pensionable earnings £
2005–06	105,600
2004–05	102,000
2003–04	99,000
2002–03	97,200
2001–02	95,400
2000–01	91,800
1999–00	90,600

Note
From 6 April 2001 the earnings cap also applies to people who contribute to stakeholder pension schemes.

Partners (ICTA 1988, s. 628)

The earned income limit for a retirement annuity paid to a former partner is 50 per cent of the average of his share of the partnership profits in the best three of the last seven years in which he was a partner.

The former partner's share of the profits in the first six of the last seven years in which he was a partner is increased by the percentage increase in the RPI from the December in the relevant year to the December in the seventh year.

Early retirement ages: retirement annuity contracts and personal pension schemes

The early retirement ages shown in the table below have been agreed generally by the Revenue under ICTA 1988, s. 620(4)(c) (retirement annuity contracts) and s. 634(3)(b) (personal pension schemes). Individuals in the professions or occupations may not normally take benefits from their pension arrangements before age 60 in the case of retirement annuity contracts and before 50 in the case of personal pension schemes, except in the case of retirement owing to illness or disability. For personal pension schemes see also Revenue booklet IR 76.

Profession or occupation	Retirement age[1] Retirement annuity contracts	Personal pension schemes
Air Pilots	55	–
Athletes (appearance and prize money)	35	35
Badminton Players	35	35
Boxers	35	35
Brass Instrumentalists	55	–
Cricketers	40	40
Croupiers	50	–
Cyclists	35	35
Dancers	35	35
Divers (Saturation, Deep Sea and Free Swimming)	40	40
Firemen (Part-time)	55	–
Fishermen (Inshore or Distant Water Trawlermen)	55	–
Footballers	35	35
Golfers (tournament earnings)	40	40
Interdealer Brokers	50	–
Jockeys – Flat Racing	45	45
– National Hunt	35	35
Martial Arts Instructors	50	–
Models	35	35
Moneybroker Dealers	50	–
Moneybroker Dealer Directors and Managers responsible for dealers	55	–
Motorcycle Riders (Motocross or Road Racing)	40	40
Motor Racing Drivers	40	40
Newscasters (ITV)	50	–
Nurses, Physiotherapists, Midwives or Health Visitors who are females	55	–
Off-Shore Riggers	50	–
Psychiatrists (who are also maximum part-time specialists employed within the National Health Services solely in the treatment of the mentally disordered)	55	–
Royal Naval Reservists	50	–
Royal Marine Reservists non-commissioned	45	45
Rugby League Players	35	35
Rugby League Referees	50	–

| Profession or occupation | Retirement age[1] | |
	Retirement annuity contracts	Personal pension schemes
Skiers (Downhill)	–	30
Singers	55	–
Speedway Riders	40	40
Squash Players	35	35
Table Tennis Players	35	35
Tennis Players (including Real Tennis)	35	35
Territorial Army Members	50	–
Trapeze Artistes	40	40
Wrestlers	35	35

Notes

[1] The pension age shown applies only to pension arrangements funded by contributions paid in respect of the relevant earnings from the occupation or profession carrying that age. If an individual wishes to make pension provisions in respect of another source of relevant earnings to which the pension age shown above does not apply then a separate arrangement, with a pension age within the normal range, must be made.

In particular, the ages shown above for professional sportsmen apply only to arrangements made in respect of relevant earnings from activities as professional sportsmen e.g. tournament earnings, appearance and prize money. They do not apply to relevant earnings from sponsorship or coaching.

State retirement pensions

| | Weekly rates | |
	Single person £	Married couple wife not a contributor £
From 11/4/05	82.05	131.20
12/4/04 to 10/4/05	79.60	127.25
7/4/03 to 11/4/04	77.45	123.80
8/4/02 to 6/4/03	75.50	120.70
9/4/01 to 7/4/02	72.50	115.90
10/4/00 to 8/4/01	67.50	107.90
12/4/99 to 9/4/00	66.75	106.70

Pension schemes updates

'Pensions Update' is a newsletter issued on an ad hoc basis. It contains guidance on new Pension Schemes Office (PSO) practices, procedures and legislation for taxpayers and their advisers. From the publication of Pensions Update 145 (24 November 2003) the newsletter is available on the Revenue's website, in PDF format (at www.inlandrevenue.gov.uk/pensionschemes/updates.htm). Earlier copies of Updates that are of current interest are also archived on the site.

Gilt-edged securities held by non-residents

From 6 April 1998, interest on all gilt-edged securities is payable gross (F(No. 2)A 1997, s. 37). Interest on gilts already in issue at that date which is payable under deduction of tax will continue to be payable net unless notice is given to the Bank of England for payment to be made gross. Interest on gilts issued since 5 April 1998 may be paid net, if the holder wishes, again by notice to the Bank of England. Payment gross does not of itself imply that the interest is exempt from tax.

Prior to 6 April 1998, certain specified gilts, and the interest payable on them, were exempt from all UK taxation as long as it was shown that they were in the beneficial ownership of persons who were not ordinarily resident in the UK (so-called FOTRA gilts). If the interest was payable under deduction of tax, that tax could be reclaimed without recourse to the terms of any applicable double tax treaty. A list of such FOTRA gilts is provided in the table below (excluding securities which have been redeemed). With effect from 6 April 1998, *all* gilt-edged securities will automatically be given FOTRA status, thereby guaranteeing exemption from tax for holders not ordinarily resident in the UK. Where income tax has been deducted from such gilts, a repayment claim (on Form A1(CNR)) may be submitted to the Inland Revenue, Centre for Non-Residents, Fitz Roy House, PO Box 46, Nottingham, NG2 1BD.

Security	Date(s) for repayment
9% Conversion Stock 2000	3 March 2000
9% Conversion Stock 2011	12 July 2011
$9^1/_2$% Conversion Stock 2001	12 July 2001
$9^3/_4$% Conversion Stock 2003	7 May 2003
Floating Rate Treasury Stock 1999	9 March 1999[1]
Floating Rate Treasury Stock 2001	8 July 2001
$2^1/_2$% Index Linked Treasury Stock 2024	Not later than 17 July 2024
$4^1/_8$% Index Linked Treasury Stock 2030	22 July 2030
$4^3/_8$% Index Linked Treasury Stock 2004	21 October 2004
$4^5/_8$% Index Linked Treasury Stock 1998	27 April 1998
$5^1/_2$% Treasury Stock 2008/12	10 September 2008 to 10 September 2012
6% Treasury Stock 1999	10 August 1999
6% Treasury Stock 2028	7 December 2028
$6^1/_4$% Treasury Stock 2010	25 November 2010
$6^1/_2$% Treasury Loan 2003	7 December 2003
$6^3/_4$% Treasury Loan 2004	26 November 2004
7% Treasury Stock 2001	6 November 2001
7% Treasury Stock 2002	7 June 2002
$7^1/_4$% Treasury Stock 2007	7 December 2007
$7^1/_2$% Treasury Stock 2006	7 December 2006
$7^1/_2$% Treasury Stock 2006	8 September 2006
$7^3/_4$% Treasury Loan 2012/15	26 January 2012 to 26 January 2015
8% Treasury Stock 2000	7 December 2000
8% Treasury Loan 2002/06	5 October 2002 to 5 October 2006
8% Treasury Stock 2003	10 June 2003
8% Treasury Stock 2013	27 September 2013
8% Treasury Stock 2015	7 December 2015

Security	Date(s) for repayment
8% Treasury Stock 2021	7 June 2021
8$\frac{1}{2}$% Treasury Loan 2000	28 January 2000
8$\frac{1}{2}$% Treasury Stock 2005	7 December 2005
8$\frac{1}{2}$% Treasury Loan 2007	16 July 2007
8$\frac{3}{4}$% Treasury Loan 2017	25 August 2017
9% Treasury Loan 2008	13 October 2008
9% Treasury Stock 2012	6 August 2012
9$\frac{1}{2}$% Treasury Loan 1999	15 January 1999
15$\frac{1}{2}$% Treasury Loan 1998	30 September 1998
3$\frac{1}{2}$% War Loan	

Notes
[1] Interest is paid by the Bank of England without deduction of UK income tax.

Individual savings accounts (ISAs)

(ITTOIA 2005, s. 694–701; and the *Individual Savings Account Regulations* 1998 (SI 1998/1870), as amended)

ISAs start on 6 April 1999 and are guaranteed to run to at least 5 April 2010.

	Maximum investment per year From 6 April 2005 £
Maxi ISA	7,000
made up of:	
Stocks and shares	up to 7,000
Cash	up to 3,000
Mini ISA types:	
Stocks and shares	4,000
Cash	3,000

	Maximum investment per year 1999–2000 to 2004–05 £
Maxi ISA	7,000
made up of:	
Stocks and shares	up to 7,000
Cash	up to 3,000
Life insurance	up to 1,000
Mini ISA types:	
Stocks and shares	3,000
Cash	3,000
Life insurance	1,000

Notes

- The Budget 2005 announced the (REV BN02) intention to extend the current linits to 5 April 2010. They were due to fall from 2006–07.

- A Maxi ISA can include a stocks and shares component, cash component and a life insurance component in a single ISA with one manager. Mini ISAs are separate ISAs, from different managers, for stocks and shares, cash and life insurance.

- Each year an individual can either start new ISAs or can put money into existing ISAs, but only into one Maxi ISA, or one Mini ISA of each type, in any particular tax year.

- To open an ISA an individual has to be aged 18 or over and resident and ordinarily resident in the UK for tax purpocoo.

- All income and gains derived from investments and life assurance policies within the account are tax free and withdrawals from the account will not attract any tax charge.

- Tax credits attached to dividends from UK companies (which from 6 April 1999 have a value of 10%) are to be paid into the ISA until 5 April 2004. There is a similar entitlement until 5 April 2004 to tax credits attached to dividends which derive from UK equities which back life assurance policies within an ISA. The life assurance company will be able to claim payment of such tax credits.

- On maturity after 5 April 1999, the capital element of a tax-exempt special savings account (TESSA) may be transferred into the cash component of an ISA. Neither the value of any TESSA held, nor the amount of any transfer on maturity, will affect the amount which can be subscribed to an ISA.

- All personal equity plans (PEPs) held at 5 April 1999 can continue to be held as PEPs, but with the same tax advantages as ISAs. TESSAs which were open at 5 April 1999 can continue to be paid into under existing rules for their full five-year life. After that date, capital from maturing TESSAs can be transferred into the cash component of an ISA.

- From 6 April 2001 cash ISAs were extended to sixteen and seventeen year olds. The overall subscription limit of £7,000 per annum was extended until April 2006.

Enterprise investment scheme (EIS)

(ICTA 1988, s. 289–312)

EIS income tax relief is given as follows:

Relief on investment	From	Amount
Maximum	2004–05	£200,000
	1998–99	£150,000
	1994–95	£100,000
	1993–94	£40,000[1]
Minimum investment	1993–94	£500
Maximum carry-back to preceding year on investments made between 6 April and 5 October	1998–99	The lower of: • 50% of the total relief in respect of the investments; and • £25,000 (£15,000 for 1994–95 to 1997–98)
Rate of relief on income tax	1993–94	20%

Note

[1] Applied to an individual's combined investment under the business expansion scheme and the enterprise investment scheme.

See p. 62 for EIS CGT reliefs.

Venture capital trusts (VCTs)

(ICTA 1988, s. 332A, 842AA, Sch. 15B; TCGA 1992, s. 151A, 151B, Sch. 5C)

A VCT is a type of investment trust, approved by the Revenue on or after 6 April 1995. Reliefs:

- in relation to shares issued up to 5 April 2004, income tax relief of 20 per cent on the amount invested, up to a maximum investment of £100,000;
- in relation to shares issued on or after 6 April 2004, income tax relief at 40 per cent on the amount invested, up to a maximum investment of £200,000; the 40 per cent relief rate will apply until at least 5 April 2006 (and should revert to the 20 per cent rate thereafter);
- provided the investment is within the limits set, investors will not be taxed on dividends received from VCT shares;
- an individual disposing of VCT shares will be exempt from capital gains tax if the acquisition costs do not exceed the investment limits in any one year;
- the IT and CGT reliefs above are subject to the condition that the investor must hold the VCT shares for at least three years (five years for shares issued prior to 6 April 2000); and
- for shares issued on or before 5 April 2004, an individual (who subscribes for new shares qualifying for income tax relief) may defer the chargeable gain which has arisen on the disposal of any asset (provided reinvestment in new VCT shares takes place within one year before and one year after the disposal); this relief ceases for shares issued on or after 6 April 2004.

To obtain the Revenue's approval, the trust must satisfy certain conditions. The main ones are as follows:

- it must be a non-close company;
- its shares must be quoted on the stock exchange;
- at least 70% of its income must be wholly or mainly derived from investments in shares or securities; and
- at least 70% (by value) of its total investments must comprise of qualifying holdings (broadly, shares in unquoted trading companies).

Lease premiums

Amount of premium assessable under Sch. A when lease is granted, where duration of lease is at least one year but not more than 50 years (ICTA 1988, s. 34 for corporation tax; ITTOIA 2005, s. 277 for income tax):

$$P \times \frac{51 - D}{50}$$

where

P   is total premium; and

D   is duration of lease in complete years (ignoring any additional part of a year).

Amount taken into account in calculating a chargeable gain will be the balance of the premium (TCGA 1992, s. 240 and Sch. 8, para. 5, 7) for which the restriction of allowable expenditure is applicable:

Length of lease in years	Amount chargeable as gains %	Amount within Sch. A %
Over 50	100	0
50	98	2
49	96	4
48	94	6
47	92	8
46	90	10
45	88	12
44	86	14
43	84	16
42	82	18
41	80	20
40	78	22
39	76	24
38	74	26
37	72	28
36	70	30
35	68	32
34	66	34
33	64	36
32	62	38
31	60	40
30	58	42
29	56	44
28	54	46
27	52	48
26	50	50
25	48	52
24	46	54
23	44	56
22	42	58
21	40	60
20	38	62
19	36	64
18	34	66
17	32	68

Length of lease in years	Amount chargeable as gains %	Amount within Sch. A %
16	30	70
15	28	72
14	26	74
13	24	76
12	22	78
11	20	80
10	18	82
9	16	84
8	14	86
7	12	88
6	10	90
5	8	92
4	6	94
3	4	96
2	2	98
1 or less	0	100

Amount of lease premium allowed as a Sch. D, Case I or II deduction:

$$\frac{\text{Schedule A charge on landlord}}{\text{D (as above)}} \times \frac{\text{Days in accounting or basis period}}{365}$$

Settlements on children

(ITTOIA 2005, s. 629)

Income paid to or for the benefit of a minor child arising from capital provided by a parent is not treated as parents' income if it does not exceed £100 per tax year.

National Savings Bank interest

Limit of income tax exemption under ITTOIA 2005, s. 691 (all years since 1977–78): £70. The exemption is available in respect of separate accounts of husband and wife. The exemption is unavailable in respect of investment deposits.

Time limits for elections and claims

In the absence of any provision to the contrary, under self-assessment for the purposes of income tax, the normal rule is that claims are to be made within five years from 31 January next following the tax year to which they relate, previously six years from the end of the relevant chargeable period (TMA 1970, s. 43(1)).

In certain cases the Board may permit an extension of the strict time limit in relation to certain elections and claims.

Provision	Time limit	Statutory reference
Set-off of loss on disposal of shares in unquoted trading company against income	12 months from 31 January following year in which loss arose	ICTA 1988, s. 574(1)
Carry-back of retirement annuity premiums	31 January next following tax year in which paid	ICTA 1988, s. 619(4)
Treat personal pension contribution as paid in preceding tax year	At or before payment made on or before 31 January in tax year	ICTA 1988, s. 641A(1)

TAXATION OF EARNINGS

Car benefit charges

Car benefit charges from 2002–03

Car benefit charges for cars with an approved CO_2 emissions figure

The benefit is calculated on a percentage of the list price of the car appropriate to the level of the car's CO_2 emissions, as follows:

- 15 per cent of the list price of cars emitting up to the lower threshold of emissions of carbon dioxide in grams per kilometre;

- increased by one per cent per 5 g/km over the lower threshold; but

- capped at 35 per cent of the list price.

The lower threshold for each year from 2002–03 is as follows (ITEPA 2003, s. 139):

Tax year	Lower threshold (in g/km)
2002–03	165
2003–04	155
2004–05	145
2005–06	140
2006–07	140 (see Note)
2007–08	140 (see Note)

Note

It was announced in Budget press release REV BN 41 (17 March 2004) that the figure of 140g/km would continue to apply for 2006–07.

It was announced in Budget press release REB BN 30 (16 March 2005) that the figure of 140g/km would continue to apply for 2007–08.

If the exact CO_2 emissions figure does not end in 0 or 5, it should be rounded *down* to the nearest 5g/km.

There is a three per cent supplement on diesel cars (subject to 35 per cent cap). No supplement is applied to diesel cars meeting the Euro IV standard, but this removal of the supplement ceases to apply from 6 April 2006 to all cars first registered from 1 January 2006.

Discounts are given for cars using alternative fuels and technologies.

CO₂ emissions in grams per kilometre (g/km)				Percentage of car's price to be taxed
2002–03	2003–04	2004–05	2005–06 to 2007–08	
165	155	145	140	15
170	160	150	145	16
175	165	155	150	17
180	170	160	155	18
185	175	165	160	19
190	180	170	165	20
195	185	175	170	21
200	190	180	175	22
205	195	185	180	23
210	200	190	185	24
215	205	195	190	25
220	210	200	195	26
225	215	205	200	27
230	220	210	205	28
235	225	215	210	29
240	230	220	215	30
245	235	225	220	31
250	240	230	225	32
255	245	235	230	33
260	250	240	235	34
265	255	245	240	35

Discounts for cars that run on alternative fuels and technologies (periods to 5 April 2006)

Type of car	Discounted charge
Battery electric cars	15% of list price, less 6% discount – i.e. 9% of list price.
Hybrid electric cars	Appropriate percentage of list price, less 2% discount and a further 1% discount for each full 20 g/km that the CO₂ emissions figure is below the lower threshold.

Type of car	Discounted charge
Cars using liquid petroleum gas (LPG) or compressed natural gas (CNG) ● Cars running on road fuel gas alone	Appropriate percentage of list price, less 1% discount and a further 1% discount for each full 20 g/km that the CO_2 emissions figure is below the lower threshold.
● Bi-fuel cars (both gas and petrol) *Cars first registered on or after 1 January 2000, and approved for running on both petrol and gas:*	Appropriate percentage of list price applying to gas CO_2 emissions, less 1% discount and a further 1% discount for each full 20 g/km that the CO_2 emissions figure is below the lower threshold.
Cars first registered before 1 January 2000, and petrol cars that are retro-fitted:	Appropriate percentage of list price applying to petrol CO_2 emissions, less 1% discount.

Discounts for cars that run on alternative fuels and technologies (from 6 April 2006)

Type of car	Discounted charge
Battery electric cars	15% of list price, less 6% discount – i.e. 9% of list price.
Bi-fuel gas and petrol cars manufactured or converted before type approval	Appropriate percentage of list price, less 2% discount
Hybrid electric and petrol cars	Appropriate percentage of list price, less 3% discount

Note: the cost of conversion is ignored for bi-fuel gas and petrol cars converted after type approval, but no additional percentage discount is given.

Car benefit charges for cars with no approved CO_2 emissions figure

This category includes all cars registered before 1 January 1998 (as no car registered before that date has an official CO_2 figure for tax purposes (ITEPA 2003, s. 134)).

The basic car benefit charge will be the car's price multiplied by the percentage charge appropriate to the car's age and engine size (including any diesel supplement).

Engine size cc	Percentage of car's price to be taxed	
	Car first registered before 1 January 1998	Car first registered on or after 1 January 1998
0–1,400	15%	15%
1,401–2,000	22%	25%
Over 2,000	32%	35%
Cars without a cylinder capacity (e.g. rotary engined petrol cars)	32%	35%

Car benefit scales 1999–2000 to 2001–02

Age of car at end of tax year under 4 years	Percentage of manufacturer's list price (maximum £80,000 price)	
	Number of cars available concurrently to employee	
	First car %	Second and subsequent cars %
Business miles		
Less than 2,500 miles	35	35
2,500 miles to 17,999 miles	25	35
18,000 miles or more	15	25
Age of car at end of tax year 4 years or more The percentages above are reduced by $\frac{1}{4}$.		

Car benefit scales 1998–99

Age of car at end of tax year under 4 years	Percentage of manufacturer's list price (maximum £80,000 price)	
	Number of cars available concurrently to employee	
	First car %	Second and subsequent cars %
Business miles		
Less than 2,500 miles	35	35
2,500 miles to 17,999 miles	$23\frac{1}{3}$	35
18,000 miles or more	$11\frac{2}{3}$	$23\frac{1}{3}$
Age of car at end of tax year 4 years or more The percentages above are reduced by $\frac{1}{3}$.		

Fuel benefit charges

From 2003–04

From 6 April 2003, the additional taxable benefit of free fuel provided for a company car is calculated using the same CO_2 figures as are used for calculating the company car charge.

For 2003–04 to 2005–06 inclusive, the CO_2 percentage figure is applied to a fixed amount of £14,400 (ITEPA 2003, s. 150(1)).

The fuel benefit is reduced to nil if the employee is required to make good the full cost of all fuel provided for private use, and does so.

A proportionate reduction is made where the company car is only available for part of the year, where car fuel ceases to be provided part way through the year, or where the benefit of the company car is shared.

Fuel benefit scales 1998–99 to 2002–03

Petrol cars

	(A) 1,400cc or less	(B) 1,401–2,000cc	(C) Over 2,000cc*
1997–98	800	1,010	1,490
1998–99	1,010	1,280	1,890
1999–2000	1,210	1,540	2,270
2000–01	1,700	2,170	3,200
2001–02	1,930	2,460	3,620
2002–03	2,240	2,850	4,200

(* and cars without an internal combustion engine)

Diesel cars

2,000cc or less: as per column (B) above.

Over 2,000cc: as per column (C) above.

Advisory fuel rates for company cars

The Revenue first published in 2002 rates that can be used for reimbursement of private mileage by company car drivers to their employers.

Engine Size	Petrol (all years)	Diesel (all years)	LPG (to 2003/04)	LPT (from 2004/05)
1400cc or less	10p	9p	6p	7p
1401cc to 2000cc	12p	9p	7p	8p
Over 2000cc	14p	12p	9p	10p

Van benefit charges

(ITEPA 2003, s. 157)

The rules changed from 6 April 2005, at which point drivers whose only private use is for ordinary commuting, and who use the van for business purposes, will be exempt. Drivers will also be exempt if private use by them (and by other members of their family and household) is 'insignificant'. Other drivers continue to pay tax on the figures above until 6 April 2007, at which point the scale charge will rise to £3,000, irrespective of the age of the van. A fuel scale charge of £500 will also apply from April 2007 for drivers paying tax on the benefit of the van itself, unless they pay for all their own private fuel.

	Age of van at end of tax year	
	Under 4 years **£**	**4 years or more** **£**
1998–99 to 2005–06	500	350

Notes

Applies to vehicles weighing up to 3.5 tonnes (ITEPA 2003, s. 115(1)).

The cash equivalent is reduced where the van is unavailable for a period of at least 30 consecutive days, or where the employee does not have use of the van at the start or end of the tax year.

Where a van is shared, the charge is reduced and a driver with limited private use can elect to pay on a benefit of £5 per day of private use.

Mileage allowance payments

Statutory mileage rates 2002–03 onwards

From April 2002, statutory rates are set for mileage allowance payments (ITEPA 2003, s. 230). An employer may reimburse business mileage at more or less than the statutory rates; any excess is taxable and any shortfall is tax deductible.

Kind of vehicle	Rate per mile
Car or van	40p for the first 10,000 miles 25p after that
Motorcycle	24p
Cycle	20p

Mileage rates up to 5 April 2002 (Fixed Profit Car Scheme)

Tax year	Tax-free rates per mile				
	Cars up to 1,000cc	Cars 1,001–1,500cc	Cars 1,501–2,000cc	Cars over 2,000cc	Composite rate[1]
2001–02					
Up to 4,000 miles	40p	40p	45p	63p	42.5p
Over 4,000 miles	25p	25p	25p	36p	25p
1997–98 to 2000–01					
Up to 4,000 miles	28p	35p	45p	63p	40p
Over 4,000 miles	17p	20p	25p	36p	22.5p

Notes

[1] Irrespective of engine size.

Transitional arrangements existed (former ICTA 1988, s. 197B) to restrict the extent to which tax liabilities on motor mileage allowances could increase from year to year.

Any employee could be taxed individually on the basis of actual motoring expenditure (the statutory basis) if necessary records were kept.

If mileage was 8,000, 4,000 miles were at each rate rather than 8,000 miles at the second rate.

Motor cycles

Tax year	Tax-free rate per mile
2000–01 to 2001–02	24p

Pedal cycles

Tax year	Tax-free rate per mile
1999–2000 to 2001–02	12p

Bus services

An exemption applies to:

(1) works transport services (ITEPA 2003, s. 242), which must be a bus or minibus:

    (a) available to employees generally;

    (b) used mainly for qualifying journeys; and

    (c) used substantially by employees or their children;

    (d) support for public bus services (ITEPA 2003, s. 243):

        (i) available to employees generally;

        (ii) used for qualifying journeys by employees of one or more employers; and

        (iii) either:

            (A) a local bus service; or

(B)   the bus must be provided to other passengers on terms that are as favourable as the terms on which the bus is provided to employees.

Mobile phones

From 1991–92 to 1998–99 inclusive, the benefit was £200 a year for each mobile telephone available for private use. No benefit arose where the employee was *required* to, and did, make good the full marginal cost of any private use.

From 6 April 1999, this charge was abolished (ITEPA 2003, s. 319).

Care is needed, as a charge can still arise in some circumstances. This will be the case if, for example, the employer reimburses the costs of calls on a privately-owned mobile phone, or buys prepayment vouchers. A charge could also arise if the employee has the right to give up the mobile phone in return for a higher salary.

Computer equipment

A limited exemption applies for computer equipment provided, without transfer of ownership, for use by employees (ITEPA 2003, s. 320):

- arrangements must not favour directors;
- first £500 of taxable benefit exempt (i.e. computer value up to £2,500, but subject to incidental expenses incurred);
- exemption can cover scanners, printers, modems, discs, etc.; but
- exemption does not apply to phone lines.

Relocation allowance

Tax relief for relocation expenses in relation to payments made or expenses provided in connection with an employee's change of residence where the employee's job or place of work is changed is generally subject to a statutory maximum of £8,000 (ITEPA 2003, s. 287).

Incidental overnight expenses and benefits

Benefits, reimbursements and expenses provided by an employer for employees' minor, personal expenditure whilst on business-related activities requiring overnight accommodation away from home are not taxable provided that the total amount reimbursed, etc. does not exceed the relevant maximum amount(s) per night, multiplied by the number of nights' absence (ITEPA 2003, s. 240). If the limit is exceeded, the whole amount provided remains taxable.

From	Authorised maximum per night	
	In UK £	Overseas £
6 April 1995	5	10

Payments on loss of office and employment

Period	Relief
From 1998–99	£30,000 exempt

Notes

The exemption is not available for any payment or other benefit chargeable to income tax under other legislation (ITEPA 2003, s. 401(3)).

There is therefore no exemption for any amounts already taxable as earnings (e.g. payments made under a contract of employment).

AA estimated running costs: general

This book used to include estimated running costs for private vehicles, reproduced by kind permission of the Automobile Association. The schedules are no longer relevant for tax purposes since the introduction from April 2002 of authorised mileage allowance payments (ITEPA 2003, s. 229).

Official rate of interest

(ITEPA 2003, s. 181)

The official rate of interest is used to calculate the cash equivalent of the benefit of an employment-related loan which is a taxable cheap loan. Since 6 April 1999, the Revenue have set a single rate in advance for the whole tax year.

The rate from 6 January 2002 is five per cent (SI 2001/3860).

It was announced in a Revenue press release dated 17 March 2005 that the five per cent rate 'will be frozen for the 2005/06 tax year, subject to review in the event of significant rate changes'. An earlier commitment was given in January 2000, that (following announcement of the rate for any given tax year) the official rate may be reduced but will not be increased in the light of interest rate changes generally. This therefore presumably means that the five per cent will not go up during the year to 5 April 2006.

For previous periods, the official rates of interest were as shown below.

Date		Rate %	SI No.
From 6 March	1999 to 5 January 2002	6.25	SI 1999/419
From 6 August	1997 to 5 March 1999	7.25	SI 1997/1681

40

The *average* official rates of interest are given below. These should be used if the loan was outstanding throughout the tax year and the normal averaging method of calculation is being used.

Year	Average official rate %
2004–05	5.00
2003–04	5.00
2002–03	5.00
2001–02	5.94
2000–01	6.25
1999–2000	6.25

Official rate of interest – foreign currency loans

The official rate of interest for certain employer-provided loans in Japanese yen or Swiss francs has been set as follows:

Loans in Swiss francs	
Date	**Rate %**
From 6 July 1994	5.5
From 6 June 1994 to 5 July 1994	5.7
Loans in Japanese yen	
Date	**Rate %**
From 6 June 1994	3.9

Note
The lower 'official rate' of interest for taxing loans in a foreign currency where interest rates in that country are significantly lower than interest rates in the UK only applies to a loan in another country's currency, to a person who normally lives in that country and has actually lived there in the year or previous five years.

Fixed sum deductions for repairing and maintaining equipment

In the case of employees required to provide tools and protective clothing because of the nature of their employment, appropriate fixed allowances have been agreed in many cases by the Revenue with trade unions.

The following table of allowances, for which employees may claim a deduction (without establishing actual expenditure) forms an appendix to ESC A1. An employee may claim actual expenditure if he can establish that it is greater.

For 2003–04 and later tax years, ITEPA 2003, s. 367 gives statutory force to ESC A1 and the fixed sum deductions will be set by the Treasury.

Manual and certain other employees: flat rate expenses deduction for tools and special clothing

Industry code	Industry	Occupation	Deduction for 1995–96 onwards £
10	Agriculture	All workers	70
100	Aluminium	a. Continual casting operators, process operators, de-dimplers, driers, drill punchers, dross unloaders, firemen, furnace operators and their helpers, leaders, mouldmen, pourers, remelt department labourers, roll flatteners	130
		b. Cable hands, case makers, labourers, mates, truck drivers and measurers, storekeepers	60
		c. Apprentices	45
		d. All other workers	100
330	Banks	Uniformed bank employees	40
90	Brass and copper	All workers	100
270	Building	a. Joiners and carpenters	105
		b. Cement works and roofing (asphalt) labourers	55
		c. Labourers and navvies	40
		d. All other workers	85
250	Building materials	a. Stone-masons	85
		b. Tilemakers and labourers	40
		c. All other workers	55
190	Clothing	a. Lacemakers, hosiery bleachers, dyers, scourers and knitters, knitwear bleachers and dyers	45
		b. All other workers	30

Industry code	Industry	Occupation	Deduction for 1995–96 onwards £
150	Constructional Engineering	a. Blacksmiths and their strikers, burners, caulkers, chippers, drillers, erectors, fitters, holders up, markers off, platers, riggers, riveters, rivet heaters, scaffolders, sheeters, template workers, turners, welders	115
		b. Banksmen labourers, shop-helpers, slewers, straighteners	60
		c. Apprentices and storekeepers	45
		d. All other workers	75
170	Electrical and Electricity supply	a. Those workers incurring laundry costs only (generally CEGB employees)	25
		b. All other workers	90
110	Engineering	a. Pattern makers	120
		b. Labourers, supervisory and unskilled workers	60
		c. Apprentices and storekeepers	45
		d. Motor mechanics in garage repair shops	100
		e. All other workers	100
40	Fire service	Uniformed fire fighters & fire officers	60
220	Food	All workers	40
20	Forestry	All workers	70
240	Glass	All workers	60
80	Healthcare	a. Ambulance staff on active service (i.e. excluding staff who take telephone calls or provide clerical support)	110
		b. Nurses and midwives, chiropodists, dental nurses, occupational speech physios and therapists, phlebotomists, radiographers	70
		c. Plaster room orderlies, hospital porters, ward clerks, sterile supply workers, hospital domestics, hospital catering staff	60
		d. Laboratory staff, pharmacists, pharmacy assistants	45
		e. Uniformed ancillary staff – maintenance workers, grounds staff, drivers, parking attendants and security guards, receptionists and other uniformed staff	45

Industry code	Industry	Occupation	Deduction for 1995–96 onwards £
280	Heating	a. Pipe fitters and plumbers	100
		b. Coverers, laggers, domestic glaziers, heating engineers and their mates	90
		c. All gas workers, all other workers	70
50	Iron Mining	a. Fillers, miners and underground workers	100
		b. All other workers	75
70	Iron and Steel	a. Day labourers, general labourers, stockmen, time-keepers, warehouse staff and weighmen	60
		b. Apprentices	45
		c. All other workers	120
210	Leather	a. Curriers (wet workers), fellmongering workers, tanning operatives (wet)	55
		b. All other workers	40
140	Particular Engineering	a. Pattern makers	120
		b. All chainmakers; cleaners, galvanisers, tinners and wire drawers in the wire drawing industry; tool-makers in the lock making industry	100
		c. Apprentices and storekeepers	45
		d. All other workers	60
355	Police Force	Uniformed police officers (ranks up to and including Chief Inspector)	55
160	Precious Metals	All workers	70
230	Printing	a. *Letterpress Section*: Electrical engineers (rotary presses), electrotypers, ink and roller makers, machine minders (rotary), maintenance engineers (rotary presses) and stereotypers	105
		b. Bench hands (P & B), compositors (lp), readers (lp), T & E Section wireroom operators, warehousemen (Ppr box)	30
		c. All other workers	70
320	Prisons	Uniformed prison officers	55

Industry code	Industry	Occupation	Deduction for 1995–96 onwards £

300	Public Service	a. *Dock and inland waterways*
		   – Dockers, dredger drivers, hopper steerers
		   – All other workers
		b. *Public transport*
		   – Garage hands (including cleaners and
		     mechanics)
		   – Conductors and drivers
			
			55
			40
			
			55
			40

60	Quarrying	All workers	70
290	Railways	(See the appropriate category for craftsmen, e.g. engineers, vehicle builders etc.) All other workers	 70

30	Seamen	a. Carpenters (Seamen) Passenger liners
		b. Carpenters (Seamen) Cargo vessels,
		   tankers, coasters and ferries
		c. Other seamen Passenger liners
		d. Other seamen Cargo vessels, tankers,
		   coasters and ferries
			165
			
			130
			nil
			
			nil

120	Shipyards	a. Blacksmiths and their strikers, boilermakers,
		   burners, carpenters, caulkers, drillers,
		   furnacemen (platers), holders up, fitters,
		   platers, plumbers, riveters, sheet iron
		   workers, shipwrights, tubers, welders
		b. Labourers
		c. Apprentices and storekeepers
		d. All other workers
			
			115
			60
			45
			75

200	Textile Prints	All workers	60
180	Textiles	a. Carders, carding engineers, overlookers (all), technicians in spinning mills b. All other workers	 85 60

130	Vehicles	a. Builders, railway wagon etc. repairers and
		   railway wagon lifters
		b. Railway vehicle painters and letterers,
		   railway wagon etc. builders' and repairers'
		   assistants
		c. All other workers
			
			105
			
			60
			40

Industry code	Industry	Occupation	Deduction for 1995–96 onwards £
260	Wood & Furniture (formerly Wood)	a. Carpenters, cabinet makers, joiners, wood carvers and woodcutting machinists	115
		b. Artificial limb makers (other than in wood), organ builders and packaging case makers	90
		c. Coopers not providing own tools, labourers, polishers and upholsterers	45
		d. All other workers	75

Note
Industry codes are Inland Revenue computer identification numbers.
'Workers' and 'all other workers' are references to manual workers or to workers who have to pay for the upkeep of tools and special clothing.

Share incentive plans

	Free shares	Partnership shares	Matching shares[4]	Divided shares[5]
Employment before eligibility	Up to 18 months employment[1]	Up to 6 months (if accumulation period); up to 18 months (if no accumulation period)[1]	Up to 6 months (if accumulation period); up to 18 months (if no accumulation period)[1]	–
Limits	Up to £3,000 per tax year	2003–04 onwards: lower of £1,500 per tax year and 10% of salary for tax year; 2000–01 to 2002–03: lower of £125 per month and 10% of monthly salary	Up to 2 matching shares for each partnership share bought	Dividends reinvested up to £1,500 in a tax year

	Free shares	Partnership shares	Matching shares[4]	Divided shares[5]
Minimum amount if stated[1]	–	At most £10 per month	–	–
Performance measures[1]	Yes	No	No	No
Holding period	At least 3 years from award[2]	None	At least 3 years from award[2]	3 years from acquisition
Forfeiture on cessation of employment[1]	Yes	No	Yes	No
Tax on award	None	None – tax relief for salary used to buy shares	None	None
Tax on removal of shares from plan within 3 years of award[3]	On market value when taken out	On market value when taken out	On market value when taken out	Original dividend taxable but in year when shares taken out of plan.
Tax on removal between 3 and 5 years of award[2]	On lower of: – value at award; and – value on removal	On lower of: – salary used to buy shares; and – value on removal	On lower of: – value at award; and – value on removal	None
Tax on removal after 5 years	None	None	None	None
CGT on removal – any time	None	None	None	None

Notes

[1] These conditions can be included at the option of the company.

[2] The holding period may be up to 5 years at the option of the company.

[3] PAYE and NICs will be operated in relation to any income tax charge where the shares are readily convertible assets.

[4] Only awarded to employees who buy partnership shares.

[5] Must be acquired with dividends from plan shares.

Approved SAYE option schemes

(ITEPA 2003 Part 7, s. 475 and Chapter 7, and Sch. 3)

No tax charge in respect of the receipt or exercise of an option where relevant conditions are met. Generally, option must be exercised more than three years after date of grant. Monthly contributions must not exceed £250 and the company may not impose a higher monthly minimum than £10.

The rules were substantially amended by FA 2003, s.139.

Company share option plans

(ITEPA 2003 Part 7, Chapter 8, and Sch. 4)

Favourable tax treatment is given where a CSOP option is exercised between three and 10 years form the date the option was granted (but subject to earlier exercises).

The maximum value of shares that can be held under option by an employee at any time is £30,000.

The price at which the option may be exercised must not be 'manifestly less' than the market value at the time the option is granted, or such earlier time as may be agreed by the Revenue and specified in the agreement.

The rules were substantially amended by FA 2003, s.139.

Approved profit sharing schemes

(ICTA 1988, s. 186, 187 and Sch. 9, 10)

Offered tax relief when shares appropriated, in the event of an increase in value of the shares, and (broadly) when gains were made on the disposal.

Income tax relief was withdrawn for awards made from the start of 2003. The rules were not re-written into ITEPA 2003.

Maximum value of shares was the greater of £3,000 or 10 per cent of salary (but capped at £8,000). Full (100 per cent) tax charge made if there was a disposal or other receipt of capital within three years of the date the shares were appropriated, but charge reduced to 50% in certain exceptional circumstances.

Enterprise management incentives (EMI)

Qualifying company	Up to 31 December 2001: gross assets not exceeding £15m From 1 January 2002: gross assets not exceeding £30m (ITEPA 2003, Sch. 5, para. 12(1))
Maximum options	Up to £100,000 per employee (ITEPA 2003, Sch. 5, para. 6)

Taxable state benefits

The following benefits are liable to income tax (ITEPA 2003, s. 577, 580, 660). Rates were updated by SI 2005/522 (The Social Security Benefits Up-rating Order 2005). See *www.dwp.gov.uk/mediacentre/pressreleases/2004/dec/rates.doc* for further details.

The site of the Social Security Agency of Northern Ireland also contains relevant information, and is better presented: *www.ssani.gov.uk/benefit_info/benefitrates.html*.

	Weekly rate from	
Benefit	**April 2005** **£**	**April 2004** **£**
Bereavement allowance	82.05	79.60
Carer's allowance	45.70	44.35
Dependent adults with retirement pension with carer's allowance with severe disablement allowance	 49.15 27.30 27.50	 47.65 26.50 26.65
Industrial death benefit: **Widow's pension** Permanent rate – higher lower	 82.05 24.62	 79.60 23.88
Invalid care allowance Standard rate	 45.70	 44.35
Incapacity benefit (long term) Rate Increase for age: 　higher rate 　lower rate	 76.45 16.05 8.05	 74.15 15.55 7.80
Jobseeker's allowance See p. 55		
Incapacity benefit (short term) Higher rate: 　under pensionable age[1] 　over pensionable age[1]	 68.20 76.45	 66.15 74.15
Non-contributory retirement pension Standard rate Age addition (at age 80)	 49.15 0.25	 47.65 0.25
Retirement pension Standard rate Age addition (at age 80)	 82.05 0.25	 79.60 0.25

Benefit	Weekly rate from	
	April 2005 £	April 2004 £
SSP, SMP, SPP and SAP See p. 54ff.		
Widow's pension[2] Pension (standard rate)	82.05	79.60
Widowed parent allowance	82.05	79.60

Notes
[1] Pensionable age is 60 for women, 65 for men. From 6 April 2020, the state pension age for women will be 65, the same as for men. From 2010, womens' state pension age will be gradually increased to bring it up to age 65 by 2020.
[2] Bereavement allowance replaced widow's pension from 9 April 2001 for all new claims by widows and widowers.

Non-taxable state benefits
- Attendance allowance
- Back to work bonus
- Child benefit
- Child maintenance bonus
- Christmas bonus
- Constant attendance allowance
- Council tax benefit
- Council tax benefit extended payment
- Criminal injuries compensation
- Disability living allowance
- Education welfare benefits
- Guardian's allowance
- Housing benefit
- Housing benefit extended payment
- Incapacity benefit (short-term – lower rate)
- Income support
- Industrial injuries disablement benefit
- Jobfinder's grant
- Jobseeker's allowance, amounts above personal or couple rate
- Lone parent's benefit run-on
- Maternity allowance
- Medical expenses incurred in the European Economic Area
- Motability
- Pneumoconiosis, byssinosis and misc. disease scheme benefits
- Reduced earnings allowance
- Statutory redundancy payments
- Retirement allowance (payable under industrial injuries scheme)

- Severe disablement allowance
- Social fund payments – budgeting loan, cold weather payment, community care grant, crisis loan, funeral payment, maternity payment, winter fuel payments
- Vaccine damage
- War disablement pension
- War pensioner's mobility supplement
- War widow's pension
- Widowed mother's allowance child dependency increase
- Winter fuel payment
- Worker's compensation (supplementation) scheme

Benefit rates

	Weekly rate from (£)	
	April 2005	April 2004
Attendance allowance		
Higher rate (day and night)	60.60	58.80
Lower rate (day or night)	40.55	39.35
Child benefit		
For the eldest qualifying child	17.00	16.55
Lone parent[4]	17.55	17.55
For each other child	11.40	11.05
Constant attendance allowance		
Exceptional rate	99.20	96.20
Intermediate rate	74.40	72.15
Normal maximum rate	49.60	48.10
Part-time rate	24.80	24.05
Exceptionally severe disablement allowance	49.60	48.10
Maternity allowance		
Standard rate	106.00	102.80
Disability living allowance (care component)		
Higher rate	60.60	58.80
Middle rate	40.55	39.35
Lower rate	16.05	15.55
Disability living allowance (mobility component)		
Higher rate	42.30	41.05
Lower rate	16.05	15.55

	Weekly rate from (£)	
	April 2005	**April 2004**
Incapacity benefit (short term)[2][4] Lower rate: under pensionable age[3] over pensionable age[3]	 57.65 73.35	 55.90 71.15

Notes

[1] Also child special allowance and child dependency increases with retirement pension, widow's benefit, short-term incapacity benefit at the higher rate and long-term incapacity benefit, invalid care allowance, severe disablement allowance, higher rate individual death benefit, unemployability supplement and short-term incapacity benefit if beneficiary over pension age.

[2] Incapacity benefit is taxable, under the *Income Tax (Earnings and Pensions) Act* 2003, except for short-term benefit payable at the lower rate. It is not taxable, however, if the recipient started receiving invalidity benefit or sickness benefit before 6 April 1995 and has continued receiving incapacity benefit since then.

[3] Pensionable age is 60 for women, 65 for men. From 6 April 2020, the state pension age for women will be 65, the same as for men. From 2010, women's state pension age will be gradually increased to bring it up to age 65 by 2020.

[4] Withdrawn from 6 July 1998 except for those who have been receiving child benefit (lone parent) since before that date and whose circumstances have not changed; or those who, since before that date, have been receiving income support or income-based jobseeker's allowance which included the lone parent rate of family premium, or a disability premium, or a pension premium, and who have just come off benefit to start work.

PAYE thresholds

	Amount	
Tax year	**Weekly £**	**Monthly £**
2005–06	94.00	408.00
2004–05	91.00	395.00
2003–04	89.00	385.00
2002–03	89.00	385.00
2001–02	87.00	378.00
2000–01	84.00	365.00
1999–00	83.00	359.60

Note

Under normal circumstances, employers need not deduct tax from employees who earn less than the above amounts.

PAYE codes

The PAYE code enables an employer or payer of pension to give the employee or pensioner the approved amount of tax-free pay.

L   tax code with basic personal allowance;

P   tax code with full personal allowance for those aged 65–74;

V   tax code with full personal allowance for those aged 65–74 plus full married couple's allowance for those aged under 75 and born before 6 April 1935. Liability is estimated at the basic rate;

Y   tax code with full personal allowance for those aged 75 or over;

T   tax code used where Inland Revenue reviewing other items in tax code. Also used where Inland Revenue asked not to use other codes;

K   total allowances are less than total deductions.

Other codes

The codes BR, DO, OT and NT are generally used where there is a second source of income and all allowances have been included in tax code which is applied to first or main source of income.

Codes A and H are no longer used (since April 2004).

PAYE returns

PAYE returns: deadlines

Forms	Date	Provision	Penalty provisions
P14, P35, P38 and P38A	19 May following tax year	*Income Tax (Pay As You Earn) Regulations* 2003 (SI 2003/2682), reg. 73, 74	TMA 1970, s. 98A
P60 (to employee)	31 May following tax year	*Income Tax (Pay As You Earn) Regulations* 2003, reg. 67	TMA 1970, s. 98A
P9D and P11D	6 July following tax year	*Income Tax (Pay As You Earn) Regulations* 2003, reg. 85	TMA 1970, s. 98
P46 (Car)	3 May, 2 August, 2 November, 2 February	*Income Tax (Pay As You Earn) Regulations* 2003, reg. 90	TMA 1970, s. 98

PAYE returns: penalties

Penalties that may be imposed for delays

Forms	Initial	Continuing	Delay exceeds 12 months
P14, P35, P38 and P38A[2]	Up to £1,200[1] per 50 employees	£100 monthly per 50 employees	Penalty not exceeding 100%[1] of the tax or NICs payable for the year of assessment but not paid by 19 April following the end of the year of assessment
Forms P9D and P11D	£300 per return[1]	£60 per day[1]	

Notes

[1] This penalty is mitigable.

[2] An automatic non-mitigable penalty applies as follows:

- up to 12 months – £100 per 50 employees chargeable for each month return delayed
- end 12 months – monthly penalty ceases to accrue; additional penalty (not fixed) to be charged

Penalties that may be imposed for incorrect returns

Forms	Provision TMA 1970	Penalty
P14, P35, P38 and P38A	s. 98A	Maximum of 100% of tax underpaid (s. 98A(4))
P9D and P11D	s. 98	Maximum penalty £3,000 (s. 98(2))

Interest on certain PAYE paid late

Where an employer has not paid the net tax deductible by him under PAYE to the collector within 14 days of the end of the tax year, the unpaid tax carries interest at the prescribed rate from the reckonable date until the date of payment. Certain repayments of tax also attract interest.

54

Payroll giving scheme

Employees whose remuneration is subject to deduction of tax at source under PAYE can make tax-deductible donations to charity by requesting that their employers deduct the donations from their pay.

Year	Maximum donation per year £
2000–01 onwards	no maximum
1996 97 to 1999–2000	1,200

Note
The Government provided a 10% supplement on all payroll giving donations for four years from 6 April 2000.

Statutory sick pay

Employers are liable to pay SSP in any period of incapacity to work to a maximum of 28 weeks at the SSP rate in force. Statutory sick pay is treated as wages and is subject to PAYE income tax and to National Insurance contributions. Statutory sick pay is not payable for certain periods in which statutory maternity pay is being paid.

The amount of SSP payable to an employee depends on the earnings band into which he or she falls. The earnings bands and the associated SSP payments are as follows:

Year to	Average gross weekly earnings	Weekly SSP rate[1]
5 April 2006	82.00 or more	68.20
5 April 2005	79.00 or more	66.15
5 April 2004	77.00 or more	64.35
5 April 2003	75.00 or more	63.25
5 April 2002	72.00 or more	62.20
5 April 2001	67.00 or more	60.20
5 April 2000	66.00 or more	59.55

Note
[1] The daily rate of SSP is ascertained by dividing the weekly rate by the number of qualifying days in the week (beginning on Sunday), then multiplying by the number of qualifying days of incapacity in the week, rounded up to the nearest penny.

Maximum entitlement

An employee reaches his maximum entitlement to SSP in one spell of incapacity when he has been paid 28 times the appropriate rate, i.e. £68.20 $\times$ 28 = £1,909.60.

Statutory maternity pay

The pay period is a maximum of 26 weeks and the period of notice that must be given to the employer is 28 days. During the first six weeks, when statutory maternity pay is payable, the earnings related rate is no longer subject to the flat rate.

Year to	First 6 weeks	Remaining weeks
From 6 April 2005	90% average weekly earnings	Lower of £106.00 or earnings related rate
From 6 April 2004	90% average weekly earnings	Lower of £102.80 or earnings related rate
From 6 April 2003[1]	90% average weekly earnings	Lower of £100.00 or earnings related rate

Note
[1] Where the maternity pay period spans 6 April 2003 there is a minimum of £75.00 a week.

2002–03 and earlier years are set out below:

Statutory maternity pay (SMP) is paid for a maximum of 18 weeks to employees with average weekly earnings of at least £75 a week (in 2002–03).

Higher weekly rate:[1]	$9/10$ of employee's average weekly earnings	
Lower weekly rate:[2]	from 6 April 2002	£75.00
	from 6 April 2001	£62.60
	from 6 April 2000	£62.20
	from 6 April 1999	£59.55

Note
[1] Payable for the first six weeks of payment.
[2] Payable for the remaining weeks of the Maternity Pay Period.

Statutory paternity pay and statutory adoption pay

Payable from April 2003 at same rate as 'remaining weeks' of maternity pay as above.

Income support and jobseeker's allowance

Rate of income support

	Weekly rate (£)	
	from April 2005	from April 2004
Single		
Under 18 usual rate	33.85	33.50
Under 18 – higher rate payable in specific circumstances	44.50	44.05
18 to 24	44.50	44.05
25 or over	56.20	55.65

	Weekly rate (£)	
	from April 2005	from April 2004
Lone parent		
Under 18 – usual rate	33.85	33.50
Under 18 – higher rate payable	44.50	44.05
18 or over	56.20	55.65
Couple		
Both under 18	33.85	33.50
Both under 18, one disabled	44.50	44.05
Both under 18, with resp. for a child	67.15	66.50
One under 18, one 18–24	44.50	44.05
One under 18, one 25+	56.20	55.65
Both 18 or over	88.15	87.30
Dependent children	43.88	42.27

Rate of jobseeker's allowance

	Weekly rate (£)	
	from April 2005	from April 2004
Contributions based JSA – personal rates		
Under 18	33.85	33.50
18 to 24	44.50	44.05
25 or over	56.20	55.65
Income based JSA – personal allowances		
Under 18	33.85	33.50
18 to 24	44.50	44.05
25 or over	56.20	55.65
Lone parent		
Under 18 – higher rate payable in specific circumstances	44.50	44.05
18 or over	56.20	55.65
Couple		
Both under 18	33.85	33.50
Both under 18, one disabled	44.50	44.05
Both under 18, with resp. for a child	67.15	66.50
One under 18, one 18–24	44.50	44.05
One under 18, one 25+	56.20	55.65
Both 18 or over	88.15	87.30

	Weekly rate (£)	
	from April 2005	from April 2004
Dependent children	43.88	42.27

Income support and jobseeker's allowance – premiums

	Weekly rate (£)	
	from April 2005	from April 2004
Premiums		
Family	16.10	15.95
Pensioner		
Single	53.25	49.80
Couple	78.90	73.65
Pensioner (higher)		
Single	53.25	49.80
Couple	78.90	73.65
Disability		
Single	23.95	23.70
Couple	34.20	33.85
Enhanced disability premium single rate	11.70	11.60
Disabled child rate	17.71	17.08
Couple rate	16.90	16.75
Severe disability		
Single	45.50	44.15
couple (lower rate)	45.50	44.15
couple (higher rate)	91.00	88.30
Disabled child	43.89	42.49
Carer	25.80	25.55
Bereavement	25.85	23.95
Allowances for personal expenses for claimants in:		
Hospital		
Higher rate	20.50	19.90
Lower rate	16.40	15.90

TAXATION OF CAPITAL GAINS

Rates, annual exemption, chattel exemption

Tax year	Annual exempt amount		Chattel exemption (max sale proceeds)[1] £	Rate	
	Individuals, PRs[2], trusts for mentally disabled £	Other trusts[3] £		Individuals[4] %	Trustees and PRs %
2005–06	8,500	4,250	6,000	10/20/40[4]	40
2004–05	8,200	4,100	6,000	10/20/40[4]	40
2003–04	7,900	3,950	6,000	10/20/40[4]	34
2002–03	7,700	3,850	6,000	10/20/40[4]	34
2001–02	7,500	3,750	6,000	10/20/40[4]	34
2000–01	7,200	3,600	6,000	10/20/40[4]	34
1999–00	7,100	3,550	6,000	20/40[5]	34

Notes

[1] Where disposal proceeds exceed the exemption limit, marginal relief restricts any chargeable gain to $5/3$ of the excess. Where there is a loss and the proceeds are less than £6,000 the proceeds are deemed to be £6,000.

[2] For year of death and next two years in the case of personal representatives (PRs) of deceased persons.

[3] Multiple trusts created by the same settlor; each attracts relief equal to the annual amount divided by the number of such trusts (subject to a minimum of 10% of the full amount).

[4] For 2000–01 onwards, capital gains taxed as top slice of income at:

- starting rate to the extent to the starting rate limit;
- lower rate to the extent above the starting rate limit but to the basic rate limit; and
- higher rate to the extent above the basic rate limit.

[5] For 1999–2000, capital gains taxed as top slice of income at:

- lower rate to the extent to the basic rate limit; and
- higher rate to the extent above the basic rate limit.

[6] For 1998–99, capital gains taxed as top slice of income at income tax rates.

Exemptions and reliefs

Taper relief

(applies to individuals, trustees and personal representatives, NOT companies)

(TCGA 1992, s. 2A and Sch. A1)

Introduced for gains realised on or after 6 April 1998. Indexation allowance to 5 April 1998 (see below) may also be available.

The chargeable gain is reduced according to how long the asset has been held or treated as held after 5 April 1998. For disposals on or before 5 April 2000, all assets acquired prior to 17 March 1998 qualify for an addition of one year to the period for which they are treated as held after 5 April 1998. For disposals on or after 6 April 2000, only non-business assets qualify for the additional year.

The taper is generally applied to the net chargeable gain for the year after deduction of any losses of the same tax year and of any losses carried forward from earlier years.

Basically, the amount of taper relief depends on:

(a)   the number of whole years in the qualifying holding period (as defined in TCGA 1992, s. 2A(8)); and

(b)   the amounts of the chargeable gain treated as:

   (i)   a gain on the disposal of a business asset; and

   (ii)   a gain on the disposal of a non-business asset.

The rules for determining the amounts of the chargeable gain that are treated as (i) a gain on the disposal of a business asset and (ii) a gain on the disposal of a non-business asset are set out in TCGA 1992, Sch. A1, para. 3.

With respect to defining a business asset, the conditions for shares to qualify as business assets are set out in TCGA 1992, Sch. A1, para. 4 and the conditions for other assets to qualify as business assets are set out in para. 5.

The tables below are in the format used in the legislation. They show the percentage of chargeable gain that is subject to capital gains tax; i.e., after taper relief. Hence, if the percentage of gain chargeable is 100 per cent, then taper relief is 0 per cent; if the percentage of gain chargeable is 95 per cent, then taper relief is 5 per cent, and so on.

Non-business assets – gains of 1998–99 onwards

Gains on non-business assets		
Number of *complete* years after 5.4.98 for which asset held	Percentage of gain chargeable	Equivalent tax rates
0	100	40/20/10
1	100	40/20/10
2	100	40/20/10
3	95	38/19/9.5
4	90	36/18/9
5	85	34/17/8.5
6	80	32/16/8
7	75	30/15/7.5
8	70	28/14/7
9	65	26/13/6.5
10 or more	60	24/12/6

Business assets – gains of 2002–03 onwards

Gains on business assets		
Number of *complete* years after 5.4.98 for which asset held	Percentage of gain chargeable	Equivalent tax rates
0	100	40/20/10
1	50	20/10/5
2 or more	25	10/5/2.5

2000–01 and 2001–02

Gains on business assets		
Number of *complete* years after 5.4.98 for which asset held	Percentage of gain chargeable	Equivalent tax rates
0	100	40/20/10
1	87.5	35/17.5/8.75
2	75	30/15/7.5
3	50	20/10/5
4 or more	25	10/5/2.5

For disposals of business assets arising in the period from 6 April 1998 to 5 April 2000, the following table applies:

Gains on business assets	
Number of *complete* years after 5.4.98 for which asset held	Percentage of gain chargeable
0	100
1	92.5
2	85
3	77.5

Note

For disposals on or after 6 April 2000, capital gains may be chargeable to capital gains tax at 40%, 20% or 10% depending on the level of total income.

Indexation allowance up to 5 April 1998 (TCGA 1992, s. 53 and 54)

Indexation allowance in respect of changes shown by the retail prices indices for months after April 1998 is allowed only for the purposes of corporation tax. For disposals made by individuals, trustees and personal representatives after April 1998, indexation allowance up to 5 April 1998 and taper relief (see above) may be obtained.

Retirement relief

(former TCGA 1992, s. 163–164 and Sch. 6)

Retirement relief exempted from CGT a certain proportion of the gain from the disposal of a business by an individual who was aged 50 and over, or who retired earlier due to ill health.

It was phased out from 6 April 1999 by a gradual reduction of the relief thresholds and ceased to be available from 6 April 2003.

The annual thresholds were as follows:

Year	100% relief on gains up to: £	50% relief on gains between: £
2003–04	none	none
2002–03	50,000	50,001–200,000
2001–02	100,000	100,001–400,000
2000–01	150,000	150,001–600,000
1999–2000	200,000	200,001–800,000

Rollover relief

(TCGA 1992, s. 152)

To qualify for rollover relief, an asset must fall within one of the 'relevant classes of assets' and the reinvestment must generally take place within the period from 12 months before to three years after the disposal of the old asset. Classes of assets qualifying for relief are as follows, but see FA 2002, Sch. 29, para 132 for the interaction of this section with the corporation tax rules for gains and losses on intangible fixed assets:

- land and buildings occupied and used exclusively for the purposes of a trade;
- fixed plant or machinery (not forming part of a building);
- ships, aricraft, hovercraft;
- satellites, space stations and spacecraft (including launch vehicles);
- goodwill;
- milk quotas, potato quotas and fish quotas;
- ewe and suckler cow premium quotas; and
- Lloyd's members' syndicate rights and assets treated as acquired, under FA 1999, s. 73, by members.

Private residence relief

(TCGA 1992, s. 222)

Relief is given on the dwelling house and on land enjoyed with the garden or grounds up to the permitted area of half a hectare, or more if required for the reasonable enjoyment of the property.

Time apportion as appropriate but last 36 months allowed in any event, as long as the property was at some time the only or main residence.

Up to £40,000 relief available where residence is partly let.

Enterprise Investment Scheme

(TCGA 1992, s. 150A)

The first disposal of shares on which relief has not been withdrawn is exempt from capital gains tax; losses arising from the first disposal of shares are eligible for relief against either income tax or capital gains tax.

Under TCGA 1992, Sch. 5B, reinvestment relief is available for gains on assets where the disposal proceeds are reinvested in new EIS shares.

Under TCGA 1992, Sch. 5BA, taper relief will be given for the gain on the first investment as though it had been owned throughout the period during which the investor remains invested in EIS companies.

See p. 27 for EIS income tax relief.

Charities

(TCGA 1992, s. 256(1))

The gains of charities are not taxable provided they are applicable, and applied, for charitable purposes only. Provisions contained in ICTA 1988, s. 505, 506 are designed to charge charities to tax on the amount of their income and gains that has not been invested, lent or spent in an approved way.

A charge to capital gains tax arises if a charity ceases to be a charity, when there is a deemed sale and reacquisition of the trust property by the trustees at market value.

Due dates

Under self–assessment:

(1)   where a tax return for the tax year was given to the taxpayer before 1 November of the following tax year, the due date of payment of capital gains tax for the tax year is **31 January of the following tax year**; and

(2)   where a tax return for the tax year was given to the taxpayer after 31 October of the following tax year, the due date of payment of capital gains tax for the tax year is **three months after the date that the tax return was given to the taxpayer**.

Leases which are wasting assets

Restrictions of allowable expenditure (TCGA 1992, s. 240 and Sch. 8, para. 1)

Fraction equal to $\dfrac{P(1) - P(3)}{P(1)}$ excluded from expenditure of TCGA 1992, s. 38(1)(a),

and fraction equal to $\dfrac{P(2) - P(3)}{P(2)}$ excluded from expenditure of TCGA 1992, s. 38(1)(b), where:

P(1) = table percentage for duration of lease at time of acquisition (or 31 March 1982 where applicable);

P(2) = table percentage for duration of lease at time expenditure incurred; and

P(3) = table percentage for duration of lease at time of disposal.

Years	%	Monthly[1] increment
50 or more	100	–
49	99.657	.029
48	99.289	.031
47	98.902	.032
46	98.490	.034
45	98.059	.036
44	97.595	.039
43	97.107	.041
42	96.593	.043
41	96.041	.046
40	95.457	.049
39	94.842	.051
38	94.189	.054
37	93.497	.058
36	92.761	.061
35	91.981	.065
34	91.156	.069
33	90.280	.073
32	89.354	.077
31	88.371	.082
30	87.330	.087
29	86.226	.092
28	85.053	.098
27	83.816	.103
26	82.496	.110
25	81.100	.116
24	79.622	.123
23	78.055	.131
22	76.399	.138
21	74.635	.147
20	72.770	.155
19	70.791	.165
18	68.697	.175
17	66.470	.186
16	64.116	.196

64

Years	%	Monthly[1] increment
15	61.617	.208
14	58.971	.221
13	56.167	.234
12	53.191	.247
11	50.038	.263
10	46.695	.279
9	43.154	.295
8	39.399	.313
7	35.414	.332
6	31.195	.352
5	26.722	.373
4	21.983	.395
3	16.959	.419
2	11.629	.444
1	5.983	.470
0	0	.499

Notes
[1] Where duration is *not* an *exact* number of years, the table percentage for the whole number of years is increased by $1/12$ of the difference between that and the next highest percentage for each odd month. Fourteen odd days or more are rounded up and treated as a month; less than 14 odd days are ignored.

Premiums for short leases – CGT/IT charge

The chart below shows the proportion of any premium received in respect of a lease of less than 50 years which is chargeable to capital gains tax and that which is chargeable to income tax (ICTA 1988, s. 34).

Length of lease in years	Amount chargeable to CGT %	Income tax Sch. A %
Over 50	100	0
50	98	2
49	96	4
48	94	6
47	92	8
46	90	10
45	88	12
44	86	14
43	84	16
42	82	18
41	80	20

Length of lease in years	Amount chargeable to CGT %	Income tax Sch. A %
40	78	22
39	76	24
38	74	26
37	72	28
36	70	30
35	68	32
34	66	34
33	64	36
32	62	38
31	60	40
30	58	42
29	56	44
28	54	46
27	52	48
26	50	50
25	48	52
24	46	54
23	44	56
22	42	58
21	40	60
20	38	62
19	36	64
18	34	66
17	32	68
16	30	70
15	28	72
14	26	74
13	24	76
12	22	78
11	20	80
10	18	82
9	16	84
8	14	86
7	12	88
6	10	90
5	8	92
4	6	94
3	4	96
2	2	98
1 or less	0	100

CGT exempt gilt-edged securities

The Revenue website contains a list of gilt-edged securities with a redemption date on or after 1 January 1992. The site states that the list will be updated 'each time a Treasury

Order is made specifying further exempt gilts.' The list may be found at *http:// www.inlandrevenue.gov.uk/cgt/gilts-list.htm*.. Any gains on such securities are not chargeable gains (TCGA 1992, s. 115(1)) and any losses are not allowable losses (TCGA 1992, s. 16(2)).

Securities may be added to the list in TCGA 1992, Sch. 9, Part II by Treasury Order. Orders made to date are:

- the *Capital Gains Tax (Gilt-Edged Securities) Order* 1993 (SI 1993/950);
- the *Capital Gains Tax (Gilt-Edged Securities) Order* 1994 (SI 1994/2656) ;
- the *Capital Gains Tax (Gilt-Edged Securities) Order* 1996 (SI 1996/1031);
- the *Capital Gains Tax (Gilt-Edged Securities) Order* 2001 (SI 2001/1122);
- the *Capital Gains Tax (Gilt-Edged Securities) Order* 2002 (SI 2002/2849); and
- the *Capital Gains Tax (Gilt-Edged Securities) Order* 2004 (SI 2004/438).
- the *Capital Gains Tax (Gilt-Edged Securities) Order* 2005 (SI 2005/276).

Stocks and bonds charged on the National Loans Funds

$2^1/_2\%$	Annuities 1905 or after
$2^3/_4\%$	Annuities 1905 or after
$2^1/_2\%$	Consolidated Stock 1923 or after
$3^1/_2\%$	War Loan 1952 or after
4%	Consolidated Loan 1957 or after
$3^1/_2\%$	Conversion Loan 1961 or after
3%	Treasury Stock 1966 or after
$2^1/_2\%$	Treasury Stock 1975 or after
$12^3/_4\%$	Treasury Loan 1992
8%	Treasury Loan 1992
10%	Treasury Stock 1992
3%	Treasury Stock 1992
$12^1/_4\%$	Exchequer Stock 1992
$13^1/_2\%$	Exchequer Stock 1992
$10^1/_2\%$	Treasury Convertible Stock 1992
2%	Index-Linked Treasury Stock 1992
$12^1/_2\%$	Treasury Loan 1993
6%	Funding Loan 1993
$13^3/_4\%$	Treasury Loan 1993
10%	Treasury Loan 1993
$8^1/_4\%$	Treasury Stock 1993
$14^1/_2\%$	Treasury Loan 1994
$12^1/_2\%$	Exchequer Stock 1994
9%	Treasury Loan 1994
10%	Treasury Loan 1994
$13^1/_2\%$	Exchequer Stock 1994
$8^1/_2\%$	Treasury Stock 1994

Stocks and bonds charged on the National Loans Funds – cont'd

$8^{1}/_{2}$%	Treasury Stock 1994 'A'
2%	Index-Linked Treasury Stock 1994
3%	Exchequer Gas Stock 1990–95
12%	Treasury Stock 1995
$10^{1}/_{4}$%	Exchequer Stock 1995
$12^{3}/_{4}$%	Treasury Loan 1995
9%	Treasury Loan 1992–96
$15^{1}/_{4}$%	Treasury Loan 1996
$13^{1}/_{4}$%	Exchequer Loan 1996
14%	Treasury Stock 1996
2%	Index-Linked Treasury Stock 1996
10%	Conversion Stock 1996
10%	Conversion Stock 1996 'A'
10%	Conversion Stock 1996 'B'
$13^{1}/_{4}$%	Treasury Loan 1997
$10^{1}/_{2}$%	Exchequer Stock 1997
$8^{3}/_{4}$%	Treasury Loan 1997
$8^{3}/_{4}$%	Treasury Loan 1997 'B'
$8^{3}/_{4}$%	Treasury Loan 1997 'C'
$8^{3}/_{4}$%	Treasury Loan 1997 'D'
$8^{3}/_{4}$%	Treasury Loan 1997 'E'
15%	Exchequer Stock 1997
7%	Treasury Convertible Stock 1997
$6^{3}/_{4}$%	Treasury Loan 1995–98
$15^{1}/_{2}$%	Treasury Loan 1998
12%	Exchequer Stock 1998
12%	Exchequer Stock 1998 'A'
$9^{3}/_{4}$%	Exchequer Stock 1998
$9^{3}/_{4}$%	Exchequer Stock 1998 'A'
$7^{1}/_{4}$%	Treasury Stock 1998 'A'
$7^{1}/_{4}$%	Treasury Stock 1998 'B'
12%	Exchequer Stock 1998 'B'
$4^{5}/_{8}$%	Index-Linked Treasury Stock 1998
$7^{1}/_{4}$%	Treasury Stock 1998
$9^{1}/_{2}$%	Treasury Loan 1999
$10^{1}/_{2}$%	Treasury Stock 1999
$12^{1}/_{4}$%	Exchequer Stock 1999
$12^{1}/_{4}$%	Exchequer Stock 1999 'A'
$12^{1}/_{4}$%	Exchequer Stock 1999 'B'
$2^{1}/_{2}$%	Index-Linked Treasury Convertible Stock 1999
$10^{1}/_{4}$%	Conversion Stock 1999
6%	Treasury Stock 1999
	Floating Rate Treasury Stock 1999
9%	Conversion Stock 2000

Stocks and bonds charged on the National Loans Funds – cont'd

9%	Conversion Stock 2000 'A'
9%	Conversion Stock 2000 'B'
9%	Conversion Stock 2000 'C'
8$^1/_2$%	Treasury Loan 2000
8%	Treasury Stock 2000
8%	Treasury Stock 2000 'A'
13%	Treasury Stock 2000
13%	Treasury Stock 2000 'A'
7%	Treasury Stock 2001
7%	Treasury Stock 2001 'A'
14%	Treasury Stock 1998–2001
2$^1/_2$%	Index-Linked Treasury Stock 2001
9$^3/_4$%	Conversion Stock 2001
10%	Treasury Stock 2001
9$^1/_2$%	Conversion Loan 2001
10%	Treasury Stock 2001 'A'
10%	Treasury Stock 2001 'B'
	Floating Rate Treasury Stock
12%	Exchequer Stock 1999–2002
12%	Exchequer Stock 1999–2002 'A'
9$^1/_2$%	Conversion Stock 2002
10%	Conversion Stock 2002
9%	Exchequer Stock 2002
7%	Treasury Stock 2002
9$^3/_4$%	Treasury Stock 2002
9$^3/_4$%	Treasury Stock 2002 'A'
9$^3/_4$%	Treasury Stock 2002 'B'
9$^3/_4$%	Treasury Stock 2002 'C'
13$^3/_4$%	Treasury Stock 2000–2003
13$^3/_4$%	Treasury Stock 2000–2003 'A'
2$^1/_2$%	Index-Linked Treasury Stock 2003
9$^3/_4$%	Conversion Loan 2003
6$^1/_2$%	Treasury Stock 2003
8%	Treasury Stock 2003
8%	Treasury Stock 2003 'A'
10%	Treasury Stock 2003
10%	Treasury Stock 2003 'A'
10%	Treasury Stock 2003 'B'
3$^1/_2$%	Funding Stock 1999–2004
11$^1/_2$%	Treasury Stock 2001–2004
9$^1/_2$%	Conversion Stock 2004
10%	Treasury Stock 2004
6$^3/_4$%	Treasury Stock 2004
5%	Treasury Stock 2004

Stocks and bonds charged on the National Loans Funds – cont'd

6³/₄%	Treasury Stock 2004 'A'
4³/₈%	Index-Linked Treasury Stock 2004
9¹/₂%	Conversion Stock 2004 'A'
12¹/₂%	Treasury Stock 2003–2005
12¹/₂%	Treasury Stock 2003–2005 'A'
10¹/₂%	Exchequer Stock 2005
9¹/₂%	Conversion Stock 2005
9¹/₂%	Conversion Stock 2005 'A'
8¹/₂%	Treasury Stock 2005
8%	Treasury Loan 2002–2006
8%	Treasury Loan 2002–2006 'A'
2%	Index-Linked Treasury Stock 2006
9³/₄%	Conversion Stock 2006
7¹/₂%	Treasury Stock 2006
7³/₄%	Treasury Stock 2006
11³/₄%	Treasury Stock 2003–2007
11³/₄%	Treasury Stock 2003–2007 'A'
7¹/₄%	Treasury Stock 2007
4¹/₂%	Treasury Stock 2007
8¹/₂%	Treasury Loan 2007
8¹/₂%	Treasury Loan 2007 'A'
8¹/₂%	Treasury Loan 2007 'B'
8¹/₂%	Treasury Loan 2007 'C'
13¹/₂%	Treasury Stock 2004–2008
9%	Treasury Loan 2008
9%	Treasury Loan 2008 'A'
9%	Treasury Loan 2008 'B'
9%	Treasury Loan 2008 'C'
9%	Treasury Loan 2008 'D'
5%	Treasury Stock 2008
2¹/₂%	Index-Linked Treasury Stock 2009
5³/₄%	Treasury Stock 2009
8%	Treasury Stock 2009
4%	Treasury Stock 2009
8%	Treasury Stock 2009 'A'
6¹/₄%	Treasury Stock 2010
4³/₄%	Treasury Stock 2010
2¹/₂%	Index-Linked Treasury Stock 2011
9%	Conversion Loan 2011
9%	Conversion Loan 2011 'A'
9%	Conversion Loan 2011 'B'
9%	Conversion Loan 2011 'C'
9%	Conversion Loan 2011 'D'
5¹/₂%	Treasury Stock 2008–2012

Stocks and bonds charged on the National Loans Funds – cont'd

9%	Treasury Stock 2012
9%	Treasury Stock 2012 'A'
5%	Treasury Stock 2012
$2^1/_2$%	Index-Linked Treasury Stock 2013
8%	Treasury Stock 2013
5%	Treasury Stock 2014
$7^3/_4$%	Treasury Loan 2012–2015
$4^3/_4$%	Treasury Stock 2015
8%	Treasury Stock 2015
8%	Treasury Stock 2015 'A'
$2^1/_2$%	Treasury Stock 1986–2016
$2^1/_2$%	Index-Linked Treasury Stock 2016
$2^1/_2$%	Index-Linked Treasury Stock 2016 'A'
12%	Exchequer Stock 2013–2017
$8^3/_4$%	Treasury Stock 2017
$8^3/_4$%	Treasury Stock 2017 'A'
$2^1/_2$%	Index-Linked Treasury Stock 2020
8%	Treasury Stock 2021
$2^1/_2$%	Index-Linked Treasury Stock 2024
5%	Treasury Stock 2025
6%	Treasury Stock 2028
$4^1/_8$%	Index-Linked Treasury Stock 2030
$4^1/_2$%	Treasury Stock 2032
2%	Index-Linked Treasury Stock 2035
$4^3/_4$%	Treasury Stock 2038

Securities issued by certain public corporations and guaranteed by the Treasury

3%	North of Scotland Electricity Stock 1989–92

Securities of negligible value

The Revenue website contains a list, constantly updated, of 'shares or securities formerly quoted (largely) on the London Stock Exchange which have been officially declared of negligible value for the purposes of a claim under s.24(2) Taxation of Chargeable Gains Act 1992.' A summary of principles, together with a link to the current list, may be found at *http://www.inlandrevenue.gov.uk/cgt/negligible_list.htm*. The time limit for a claim is two years from the end of the tax year (or accounting period of a company) in which the deemed disposal and reacquisition take place.

Identification of securities

Pooling for capital gains tax (but not corporation tax) ceased for acquisitions made on or after 6 April 1998.

Disposals made on or after 6 April 1998 are identified with acquisitions in the following order (TCGA 1992, s. 105, s. 105A and s. 106A):

(1) shares acquired on the same day as the disposal (TCGA 1992, s. 105(1)), but subject to the effect of an election made under TCGA 1992, s. 105A (see below);

(2) shares acquired within 30 days following the disposal, on a FIFO (First In First Out) basis;

(3) shares acquired after 5 April 1998, on a LIFO (Last In First Out) basis;

(4) shares in a 'section 104' holding, as defined in TCGA 1992, s. 104(3);

(5) shares in a 1982 holding, as defined in TCGA 1992, s. 109(1); and

(6) shares acquired before 6 April 1965.

Under TCGA 1992, s. 105A, an election can be made for approved-scheme shares, as defined in that section, to be treated as a separate holding from that of the other shares acquired on the same day as the disposal. The time limit for the election is set out in TCGA 1992, s. 105B(2). Where the election has been made, the holding of the approved-scheme shares is identified, with the disposal, after the holding of the other shares acquired on the same day.

Expenses incurred by personal representatives
(SP 2/04)

In respect of deaths after 5 April 2004, the scale of expenses allowable in computing the gains or losses of personal representatives on the sale of assets in a deceased person's estate is as follows:

Gross value of estate	Allowable expenditure
Up to £50,000	1.8% of probate value of assets sold by personal representatives
£50,001–£90,000	£900, divided among all assets in the estate in proportion to their probate values and allowed in those proportions on assets sold by personal representatives
£90,001–£400,000	1% of probate value of assets sold
£400,001–£500,000	£4,000, divided as above
£500,001–£1,000,000	0.8% of probate value of assets sold
£1,000,001–£5,000,000	£8,000, divided as above
Over £5,000,000	Negotiated with the inspector

Note
Computations based either on the above scale or on actual expenditure incurred are accepted.

In respect of deaths after 5 April 1993 but before 6 April 2004, under SP 8/94 the scale of expenses allowable in computing the gains or losses of personal representatives on the sale of assets in a deceased person's estate is as follows:

Gross value of estate	Allowable expenditure
Up to £40,000	1.75% of probate value of assets sold by personal representatives
£40,001–£70,000	£700, divided among all assets in the estate in proportion to their probate values and allowed in those proportions on assets sold by personal representatives
£70,001–£300,000	1% of probate value of assets sold
£300,001–£400,000	£3,000, divided as above
£400,001–£750,000	0.75% of probate value of assets sold
Over £750,000	Negotiated with the inspector

Note
Computations based either on the above scale or on actual expenditure incurred are accepted.

Time limits for elections and claims

In the absence of any specific provision to the contrary, under self-assessment the normal rule is that claims are to be made within five years from 31 January next following the year to which they relate, otherwise the limit is six years from the end of the relevant chargeable period (TMA 1970, s. 43(1)).

In certain cases the Board *may* permit an extension of the strict time limit in relation to certain elections and claims.

Provision	Time limit	References
Post-cessation expenses relieved against gains	12 months from 31 January next following the tax year in which expenses paid	ICTA 1988, s. 109A
Trading losses relieved against gains	12 months from 31 January next following the tax year loss arose	ICTA 1988, s. 380; FA 1991, s. 72
Value of asset negligible	2 years from end of tax year (or accounting period if a company) in which deemed disposal/ reacquisition takes place	TCGA 1992, s. 24(2)
Re-basing of all assets to 31 March 1982 values	Within 12 months from 31 January next following the tax year of disposal (or 2 years from end of accounting period of disposal if a company)	TCGA 1992, s. 35(6)
50% relief if deferred charge on gains before 31 March 1982	Within 12 months from 31 January next following the tax year of disposal (or 2 years from end of accounting period of disposal if a company)	TCGA 1992, s. 36 and Sch. 4, para. 9(1)

Provision	Time limit	References
Variation within 2 years of death not to have CGT effect	6 months from date of variation (election not necessary for variations on or after 1 August 2002)	TCGA 1992, s. 62(7)
Specifying which "same day" share acquisitions (through employee share schemes) should be treated as disposed of first	Date of earliest disposal	TCGA 1992, s. 105A
Replacement of business assets (roll-over relief)	5 years from 31 January next following the tax year (or 6 years from the end of the accounting period if a company) Replacement asset to be purchased between 12 months before and 3 years after disposal of old asset	TCGA 1992, s. 152(1)
Disapplication of incorporation relief under TCGA 1992, s. 162	2 years from 31 January following the end of the year of assessment in which the business is transferred	TCGA 1992, s. 162A
Disposal of asset and re-investment in qualifying company (prior to 30 November 1993, applied only to disposal of qualifying shares or securities) (re-investment relief) (repealed for 1998–99 onwards)	5 years from 31 January next following the tax year	Former TCGA 1992, s. 164A(2)
Hold-over of gain on gift of business asset	5 years from 31 January next following the tax year	TCGA 1992, s. 165(1)
Determination of main residence	2 years from acquisition of second property (see ESC D21)	TCGA 1992, s. 222(5)
Irrecoverable loan to a trader	2 years from end of tax year (or accounting period if a company) otherwise effective from date claimed (see SP 8/90)	TCGA 1992, s. 253(3)
Retirement relief: ill-health grounds (pre 2003–04)	12 months from 31 January next following the year of assessment in which the disposal occurred	Former TCGA 1992, Sch. 6, para. 5(2)

INHERITANCE TAX

Lifetime transfers

(IHTA 1984, s. 7, Sch. 1)

Gross cumulative total £	Gross rate of tax %	Net cumulative total £	Tax on each £ *over* net cumulative total for grossing up
After 5 April 2005			
275,000	Nil	275,000	$\frac{1}{4}$
Over 275,000	20	–	–
After 5 April 2004			
263,000	Nil	263,000	$\frac{1}{4}$
Over 263,000	20	–	–
After 5 April 2003			
255,000	Nil	255,000	$\frac{1}{4}$
Over 255,000	20	–	–
6 April 2002–5 April 2003			
250,000	Nil	250,000	$\frac{1}{4}$
Over 250,000	20	–	–
6 April 2001–5 April 2002			
242,000	Nil	242,000	$\frac{1}{4}$
Over 242,000	20	–	–
6 April 2000–5 April 2001			
234,000	Nil	234,000	$\frac{1}{4}$
Over 234,000	20	–	–
6 April 1999–5 April 2000			
231,000	Nil	231,000	$\frac{1}{4}$
Over 231,000	20	–	–

Note

FA 2005, s. 98 sets the limits for 2006–07 at £285,000 and for 2007–08 at £300,000.

Transfers on death or within seven years before death on or after 18 March 1986

Where a person dies on or after 18 March 1986, his estate and all chargeable transfers made within seven years before his death are subject to inheritance tax (CTT if before 25 July 1986) at the rates set out below. There is a tapered reduction in the tax payable on transfers between seven and three years before death.

Gross cumulative total £	Gross rate of tax %	Net cumulative total £	Tax on each £ *over* net cumulative total for grossing up
After 5 April 2005			
275,000	Nil	275,000	$^2/_3$
Over 275,000	40	–	–
After 5 April 2004			
263,000	Nil	263,000	$^2/_3$
Over 263,000	40	–	–
After 5 April 2003			
255,000	Nil	255,000	$^2/_3$
Over 255,000	40	–	–
6 April 2002–5 April 2003			
250,000	Nil	250,000	$^2/_3$
Over 250,000	40	–	–
6 April 2001–5 April 2002			
242,000	Nil	242,000	$^2/_3$
Over 242,000	40	–	–
6 April 2000–5 April 2001			
234,000	Nil	234,000	$^2/_3$
Over 234,000	40	–	–
6 April 1999–5 April 2000			
231,000	Nil	231,000	$^2/_3$
Over 231,000	40	–	–

Note
FA 2005, s. 98 sets the limits for 2006–07 at £285,000 and for 2007–08 at £300,000.
The above scales apply to lifetime transfers made within seven years before death. For the tapered reduction in tax payable on transfers made between seven and three years before death, see p. 78.

Exemptions

Annual and small gift exemption

(IHTA 1984, s. 19, 20)

	On or after 6 April 1981 £	6 April 1980 to 5 April 1981 £	6 April 1976 to 5 April 1980 £
Annual	3,000	2,000	2,000
Small gift	250	250	100

Gifts in consideration of marriage

(IHTA 1984, s. 22)

Donor	Exemption limit £
Parent of party to the marriage	5,000
Remote ancestor of party to the marriage	2,500
Party to the marriage	2,500
Any other person	1,000

Gift by UK-domiciled spouse to non-UK domiciled spouse

(IHTA 1984, s. 18)

Transfer on or after	Exemption limit £
9 March 1982	55,000

Reliefs

Agricultural and business property relief

Type of relief	Rate of relief for disposals			
	before 10/3/92 %	10/3/92– 31/8/95 %	1/9/95– 5/4/96 %	on or after 6/4/96 %
Agricultural property (IHTA 1984, s. 115ff.)[1]				
Vacant possession or right to obtain it within 12 months	50	100	100	100
Tenanted land with vacant a possession value	50	100	100	100
Entitled to 50% relief at 9 March 1981 and not since able to obtain vacant possession	50	100	100	100
Agricultural land let on or after 1 September 1995	N/A	N/A	100	100
Other circumstances	30	50	50	50
Business property (IHTA 1984, s. 103ff.)				
Nature of property				
Business or interest in business	50	100	100	100
Controlling shareholding in quoted company	50	50	50	50
Controlling shareholding in unquoted[2] company	50	100	100	100
Settled property used in life tenant's business	50/30[3]	100/50[3]	100/50[3]	100/50[3]
Shareholding in unquoted[2] company: more than 25% interest	50[4]	100	100	100
Minority shareholding in unquoted[2] company: 25% or less	30[5]	50	50	100
Land, buildings, machinery or plant used by transferor's company or partnership	30	50	50	50

Notes
[1] From 6 April 1995, short rotation coppice is regarded as agricultural property.
[2] With effect from 10 March 1992 'unquoted' means shares not quoted on a recognised stock exchange and therefore includes shares dealt in on the Unlisted Securities Market (USM) or Alternative Investment Market (AIM).
[3] The higher rate applies if the settled property is transferred along with business itself (*Fetherstonhaugh & Ors v IR Commrs* [1984] BTC 8,046).
[4] 30% if a minority interest transferred before 17 March 1987, or if transferor had not held at least 25% interest throughout preceding two years.
[5] The relief was 20% for transfers after 26 October 1977 but before 15 March 1983.

Quick succession relief

Years between transfers More than	Not more than	Percentage applied to formula below
0	1	100
1	2	80
2	3	60
3	4	40
4	5	20

Formula

Tax charge on earlier transfer $\times \dfrac{\text{Increase in transferee's estate}}{\text{Diminution in transferor's estate}}$

Instalment option

Interest-free:

Controlling shareholdings. Holdings of 10% or more of unquoted shares with value over £20,000. Certain other death transfers of unquoted shares. Business or interest in business. Agricultural value of agricultural property. Woodlands.

Not interest-free:

Land, wherever situated, other than within categories above. Shareholdings in certain land investment and security dealing companies, or market makers or discount houses.

Fall in value relief

Type of property	Period after death
Quoted securities sold	One year
Qualifying investments cancelled or whose quotations suspended – deaths after 15 March 1992	One year
Interests in land – deaths after 15 March 1990	Four years
Interests in land – deaths before 16 March 1990	Three years

Taper relief

Years between gift and death More than	Not more than	Percentage of full tax charge at death – rates actually due %
3	4	80
4	5	60
5	6	40
6	7	20

Delivery of accounts

Nature of transfer	Due Date
Chargeable lifetime transfer	Later of: – 12 months after end of month in which transfer occurred – 3 months after person became liable
Potentially exempt transfers which have become chargeable	12 months after end of month in which death of transferor occurred
Transfers on death	Later of: – 12 months after end of month in which death occurred – 3 months after personal representatives first act or have reason to believe an account is required
Gifts subject to reservation included in donor's estate at death	12 months after end of month in which death occurred
National heritage property	6 months after end of month in which chargeable event occurred

Values below which no account required

Excepted lifetime chargeable transfers on and after 1 April 1981	£
Transfer in question, together with all other chargeable transfers in same 12-month period ending on 5 April	10,000
Transfer in question, together with all previous chargeable transfers during preceding ten years	40,000

Excepted estates

Domiciled in the United Kingdom

Deaths on and after	But before	Total gross value(1) £	Total gross value of property outside UK £	Total value of settled property £	Aggregate value of 'specified transfers' £
6 April 2003	–	240,000	75,000	100,000	100,000
6 April 2002	6 April 2003	220,000	75,000	100,000	100,000
6 April 2000	6 April 2002	210,000	50,000	–	75,000
6 April 1998	5 April 2000	180,000	30,000	–	50,000
6 April 1996	5 April 1998	180,000	30,000	–	50,000
6 April 1995	5 April 1996	145,000	15,000	–	–
1 April 1991	6 April 1995	125,000	15,000	–	–
1 April 1990	1 April 1991	115,000	15,000	–	–
1 April 1989	1 April 1990	100,000	15,000	–	–
1 April 1987	1 April 1989	70,000	10,000	–	–

Note

(1) For deaths on or after 6 April 2002 the limit applies to the aggregate of the gross value of the estate *plus* the value of 'specified transfers' which is extended and includes chargeable transfers, within seven years prior to death, of cash, quoted shares or securities, **or an interest in land and furnishings and chattels disposed of at the same time to the same person** (excluding property transferred subject to a reservation or property which becomes settled property).

For deaths on or after 6 April 1996 but before 6 April 2002 this limit applies to the total gross value of the estate *plus* the value of any transfers of cash or of quoted shares or securities made within seven years before death.

Penalties for failure in relation to obligations falling due between 26 July 1999 and 22 July 2004

Failure to deliver an IHT account (IHTA 1984, s. 216)	Account outstanding at end of statutory period	Up to £100 (but not exceeding tax due)
	Daily penalty after failure declared by a court or the special commissioners	Up to £60 a day
	Further penalty after six months from end of statutory period, if proceedings for declaring the failure not started before then	Up to £100 (but not exceeding tax due)

Failure by professional person to deliver a return of a settlement by a UK-domiciled person but with non-resident trustees (IHTA 1984, s. 218)	Account outstanding at end of statutory period (three months from making of settlement)	Up to £300
	Daily penalty after failure declared by a court or the special commissioners	Up to £60 a day
Failure to comply with a notice requiring information (IHTA 1984, s. 219)	Penalty	Up to £300
	Daily penalty after failure declared by a court or the special commissioners	Up to £60 a day
Failure to comply with a notice requiring documents, accounts or particulars (IHTA 1984, s. 219A)	Penalty	Up to £50
	Daily penalty after failure declared by a court or the special commissioners	Up to £30 a day
Incorrect information provided by persons liable to tax (IHTA 1984, s. 247)	Fraud	Up to £3,000 plus the amount of the extra tax
	Negligence	Up to £1,500 plus the amount of the extra tax
Incorrect information provided by others (IHTA 1984, s. 247)	Fraud	Up to £3,000
	Negligence	Up to £1,500
Person assisting in providing incorrect information etc. (IHTA 1984, s. 247)	Penalty	Up to £3,000

Penalties for failure in relation to obligations falling due after 22 July 2004

Failure to deliver an IHT account (IHTA 1984, s. 216)	Account outstanding at end of statutory period	Fixed penalty of £100 (but not exceeding tax due)[1]
	Daily penalty after failure declared by a court or the special commissioners	Up to £60 a day
	Penalty after six months from end of statutory period, if proceedings for declaring the failure not started before then	Fixed penalty of £200 (but not exceeding tax due)[1]
	Penalty after twelve months from end of statutory period where tax is payable	Up to £3,000[2]
Failure by professional person to deliver a return of a settlement by a UK-domiciled person but with non-resident trustees (IHTA 1984, s. 218)	Account outstanding at end of statutory period (three months from making of settlement)	Up to £300
Failure to report a deed of variation which increases the IHT liability (IHTA 1984, s. 218A)	Penalty for failure to report within 18 months of deed of variation being executed	Up to £3,000[3]
	Daily penalty after failure declared by a court or the special commissioners	Up to £60 a day
Failure to comply with a notice requiring information (IHTA 1984, s. 219)	Penalty	Up to £300
	Daily penalty after failure declared by a court or the special commissioners	Up to £60 a day
Failure to comply with a notice requiring documents, accounts or particulars (IHTA 1984, s. 219A)	Penalty	Up to £50

	Daily penalty after failure declared by a court or the special commissioners	Up to £30 a day
Incorrect information provided by persons liable to tax (IHTA 1984, s. 247)	Fraud or negligence	Up to the amount of the extra tax[4]
Incorrect information provided by others (IHTA 1984, s. 247)	Fraud or negligence	Up to £3,000[4]
Person assisting in providing incorrect information etc. (IHTA 1984, s. 247)	Penalty	Up to £3,000

Notes
[1] The change does not take effect until 23 January 2005.
[2] The change applies where the due date for delivery of an account expires after 22 July 2004. Where the due date has expired before 22 July 2004, the penalty does not apply until 23 July 2005. The penalty is subject to the defence of reasonable excuse.
[3] The change applies where the due date for notification expires after 22 July 2004. Where the due date has expired before 22 July 2004, the penalty does not apply until 23 July 2005.
[4] These changes take effect for accounts, information and documents delivered after 22 July 2004.

Due dates for payment

Transfer	Due Date
Chargeable lifetime transfers between 6 April and 30 September	30 April in following year
Chargeable lifetime transfers between 1 October and 5 April	6 months after end of month in which transfer made
Potentially exempt transfers which become chargeable	6 months after end of month in which death occurred
Transfers on death; extra tax payable on chargeable lifetime transfers within seven years before death	6 months after end of month in which death occurred

Prescribed rates of interest

(IHTA 1984, s. 233)

Interest is charged at the following rates on late payments or repayments of inheritance tax or capital transfer tax.

84

Dates at which rates applicable	Chargeable transfers made on death %	Chargeable transfers not made on death %	Source
From 6 September 2004	4	4	(1)
6 December 2003 to 5 September 2004	3	3	(1)
6 August 2003 to 5 December 2003	2	2	(1)
6 November 2001 to 5 August 2003	3	3	(1)
6 May 2001 to 5 November 2001	4	4	(1)
6 February 2000 to 5 May 2001	5	5	(1)
6 March 1999 to 5 February 2000	4	4	(1)

Note
(1) Rate change by order under the *Taxes (Interest Rate) Regulations* 1989 (SI 1989/1297).

TAXATION OF COMPANIES

Corporation tax rates

The rates of corporation tax for recent financial years are given below:

Financial year	Full rate %	Small companies' rate %	Profit limit for small companies' rate (lower limit)	Profit limit for small companies' marginal relief (upper limit)	Marginal relief fraction for small companies	Starting rate %	Profit limit for starting rate (lower limit)	Profit limit for starting rate marginal relief (upper limit)	Marginal relief fraction for starting rate
2005	30	19	300,000	1,500,000	11/400	0	10,000	50,000	19/400
2004	30	19	300,000	1,500,000	11/400	0	10,000	50,000	19/400
2003	30	19	300,000	1,500,000	11/400	0	10,000	50,000	19/400
2002	30	19	300,000	1,500,000	11/400	0	10,000	50,000	19/400
2001	30	20	300,000	1,500,000	1/40	10	10,000	50,000	1/40
2000	30	20	300,000	1,500,000	1/40	10	10,000	50,000	1/40
1999	30	20	300,000	1,500,000	1/40	–	–	–	–

Notes

(1) The lower and upper limits for the small companies' rate and the small companies' marginal relief, as well as the similar lower and upper limits for the starting rate, are reduced proportionally:

● for accounting periods of less than 12 months, and

● in the case of associated companies, by dividing the limits by the total number of non-dormant associated companies.

(2) With effect for distributions made on or after 1 April 2004, the benefit of the starting rate and marginal starting rate relief applies only to undistributed profits and profits distributed to other companies. Profits chargeable to corporation tax below the threshold for the small companies' rate that have been distributed to non-company shareholders are subject to a minimum rate (the 'non-corporate distribution rate': NCD rate which, for the financial years 2004 and 2005, is equivalent to the small companies' rate). Profits distributed to other bodies subject to corporation tax are disregarded for the purpose of establishing whether the NCD rate applies.

(3) 'Close investment holding companies' do not receive the benefit of the small companies' rate or the starting rate and so are taxable entirely at the full rate regardless of the level of their profits.

Effective marginal rates

For marginal small companies' relief and marginal starting rate relief, there is an effective rate of tax in the margin, i.e. between the lower and upper limits given for each in the preceding table, which *exceeds* the full rate. These marginal rates are not prescribed by statute, but are derived from the appropriate corporation tax rates and fractions. The applicable rates are as follows.

Financial year	Marginal small companies' rate %	Marginal starting rate %
2005	32.75	23.75
2004	32.75	23.75

Financial year	Marginal small companies' rate %	Marginal starting rate %
2003	32.75	23.75
2002	32.75	23.75
2001	32.5	22.5
2000	32.5	22.5
1999	32.5	–

Marginal relief (ICTA 1988, s. 13)

$$\text{Deduction} = (\text{Upper Limit} - \text{Profits}) \times \frac{\text{Basic profits}}{\text{Profits}} \times \text{Marginal Relief Fraction}$$

'Profits' means profits as finally computed for corporation tax purposes *plus* franked investment income *excluding* franked investment income from companies in the same group (distributions are treated as coming from within the group if the dividends so received are group income or would be group income if the companies so elected or, for distributions made on or after 6 April 1999, if the distributions are received from a company which is a 51 per cent subsidiary or a consortium company, the recipient being a member of the consortium) *plus* foreign income dividends (up to 5 April 1999).

'Basic profits' means profits as finally computed for corporation tax purposes (also known as 'profits chargeable to corporation tax').

Similar provisions apply for calculating marginal relief for the starting rate effective from 1 April 2000.

Advance corporation tax

ACT is abolished for distributions made on or after 6 April 1999 and ceases to be payable with effect from that date.

Following abolition of the requirement for companies to account for ACT, there are restrictions to tax relief for surplus unutilised ACT at that date.

Charge on loans to participators

(ICTA 1988, s. 419)

For loans or advances made on or after 6 April 1999, the rate of charge is determined under ICTA 1988, s. 419(1). This is fixed at 25 per cent of the amount of the loan or advance until further notice.

The charge itself is separate from other liabilities, being treated 'as if it were an amount of corporation tax chargeable on the company'.

Due and payable dates

For accounting periods ending on or after 1 July 1999.

Liability	Due date
Mainstream tax (TMA 1970, s. 59D)	Nine months and one day after end of an accounting period
Mainstream tax in instalments[1]:	
• instalments	The 14th day of the seventh, tenth, 13th and 16th months after start of a 12 month accounting period.
• balance after instalments	Nine months and one day after end of an accounting period.
Income tax on interest, annual payments etc.	14 days after end of return period.[2]
Charge on loans to participators (ICTA 1988, s. 419)	Nine months and one day after the end of the accounting period in which the loan was advanced.

Notes

[1] TMA 1970, s. 59E and SI 1998/3175 provide for the payment of corporation tax by 'large' companies (defined in accordance with the small companies' marginal relief upper limit) in instalments. The system is phased in over a four-year period with 60 per cent, 72 per cent and 88 per cent of a large company's liability in the first, second and third year of the change being payable in instalments.

Companies which are 'large' because of the number of associated companies or because of substantial dividend income will not have to pay by instalments if their corporation tax liabilities are less than £10,000 (for accounting periods ending after 30 June 2000; previously the limit was £5,000). Companies which become 'large' in an accounting period, having previously had profits below the upper limit, may be exempt from instalment arrangements in certain circumstances. Groups containing 'large' companies are able to pay corporation tax on a group-wide basis.

For accounting periods ending after 30 June 2005, corporation tax and the supplementary charge payable by oil companies on ring fence profits are payable in three equal instalments. Corporation tax due on other profits (i.e. non-ring fence) continues to be payable in quarterly instalments as above.

The payment dates for the three instalments once the transitional period (see below) has passed are as follows:

(1)   one-third payable six months and 13 days from the start of the accounting period (unless the date for instalment (3) is earlier);

(2)   one-third payable three months from the first instalment due date (unless (3) is earlier); and

(3)   the balance payable 14 days from the end of the accounting period (regardless of the length of the period). Transitional arrangements apply for the first accounting period affected. These arrangements leave the first two quarterly instalments unchanged (at one-quarter each of the estimated liability for the period) but then require payment of the remainder of the estimated liability on ring fence profits for that accounting period to be paid on the new third instalment date.

[2] Return periods end on 31 March, 30 June, 30 September, 31 December and at the end of an accounting period. The requirement for companies to deduct and account for income tax on certain payments is removed with effect for payments after 31 March 2001 of:

•   interest, royalties, annuities and other annual payments made to companies withing the charge to UK corporation tax on that income; and

•   interest on quoted Eurobonds paid to non–residents.

Filing deadlines

(FA 1998, Sch. 18, para. 14 for accounting periods ending on or after 1 July 1999)

The filing date for a return of profits (CT 600, or approved substitute) is generally the later of the three dates outlined below. Note that only the first two of these are relevant unless the company is making a return in respect of an accounting period forming part of a period of account which is greater than 12 months in length.

- 12 months from the end of the return period.
- Three months after the issue of a notice to deliver a corporation tax return.
- If a period of account is greater than 12 months in length, it will be divided into two or more accounting periods.

  If such a period of account is no longer than 18 months, the filing date for both accounting periods is 12 months from the end of the period of account.

  If such a period of account is greater than 18 months, the filing date for the first accounting period is 30 months from the start of the period of account. The date for the second and any subsequent accounting period is 12 months from the end of that accounting period.

Notes

Obligation to file a return is not automatic but is imposed by notice issued by the inspector.

Where a company is not sent a notice, and has not submitted a return, it must notify the Revenue of its chargeability within 12 months of the end of the accounting period. Failure to do so can result in a penalty.

In any case, tax due for an accounting period should be paid by the due date.

An amended return under self assessment may not be made later than 12 months after the filing date stipulated above.

Penalties

Infringement penalised	Maximum penalty	Provision	
		TMA 1970	FA 1998, Sch. 18
Failure to notify chargeability	100% of tax unpaid 12 months after end of accounting period	s. 10(3)	para. 2
Failure to make return • up to 3 months after filing date • more than 3 months after filing date	*Fixed rate penalty*[1] £100 (persistent failure, £500) £200 (persistent failure, £1,000)	s. 94(1), (5)	para. 17(2), (3)
• at least 18 months but less than 24 months after end of return period • 24 months or more after end of return period	*Tax-geared penalty*[2] 10% of tax unpaid at 18 months after end of return period 20% of tax unpaid at 18 months after end of return period	s. 94(6)	para. 18
Fraudulent or negligent submission of an incorrect return or accounts	100% of tax lost	s. 96	para. 20, 89
Failure to keep and preserve records (subject to specific exceptions)	Up to £3,000	–	para. 23
Failure to produce documents for purposes of an enquiry	£50 plus penalty for continued failure of £30 per day (£150 per day if determined by commissioners)	–	para. 29

Notes
[1] Fixed rate penalty does not apply if return filed by date allowed by Registrar of Companies.
[2] Tax geared penalty is charged in addition to fixed penalty. Where more than one tax–geared penalty is incurred the total penalty shall not exceed the largest individual penalty on that tax.

Interest on overdue tax

Interest on	Interest runs from	Provision in TMA 1970
Overdue corporation tax	Date tax due and payable (nine months and one day after end of accounting period)[1]	s. 87A
Corporation tax payable in instalments	Date instalment is due to be paid	s. 87A (as amended by SI 1998/3175)

Interest on	Interest runs from	Provision in TMA 1970
Overdue income tax deducted from certain payments[2]	14 days after end of return period	s. 87
Overdue ACT	14 days after end of return period	s. 87
Overdue tax due on loans to participators	Date tax due and payable	s. 109

Notes

[1] Where one group company is liable to interest and another group company with the same accounting period is due a repayment of corporation tax an election may be made for the overpayment to be surrendered so as to reduce the interest liability of the first company which will be treated as having paid tax at the same time as the surrendering company (FA 1989, s. 102).

[2] Interest provisions cease to apply to ACT for accounting periods beginning on or after 6 April 1999 following abolition of ACT.

Interest on overpaid tax

Repayment interest on corporation tax runs from later of:

(1) due and payable date (nine months after end of accounting period); and

(2) date of actual payment; except for

(a) overpayments of instalments of corporation tax, when interest runs from the first instalment date on which the excess amount would have been due and payable or, if later, the date on which that excess arises; and

(b) for companies outside the instalments regime, if tax was paid earlier than the normal due date, then interest on repayments in advance of agreement of liability runs from the first instalment date on which the excess amount would have been due and payable had the instalments regime applied or, the date on which the amount repayable was originally paid, whichever is later.

Interest on repayments of income tax deducted at source from income will run from the day after the end of the accounting period in which the income was received for accounting periods under self assessment.

Rates of interest on overdue tax

With effect for **interest** periods commencing on 6 February 1997, the rates of interest for the purposes of late paid or unpaid corporation tax are different from those for other taxes. From that date, the rate of interest on late paid or unpaid corporation tax will depend on the accounting period for which the tax is due and, under self assessment, the nature of the tax due:

Self assessment

For accounting periods within the self assessment regime (or CTSA – APs ending on or after 1 July 1999), these rates are distinct from those for periods before the start of self assessment because the interest is an allowable deduction for tax purposes (see below).

In addition, there are separate provisions for:

- overpaid instalments of corporation tax (which benefit from a more favourable rate – for details of payment by instalments, see below); and
- other liabilities such as the final liability due on the date specified in accordance with the table below.

Pre-self assessment

For accounting periods before the start of self assessment, there are two rates of interest applicable to all unpaid/late paid tax depending on whether the accounting period is within the Pay and File regime (APs ending after 30 September 1993) or not (i.e. periods ending before 1 October 1993).

CTSA (APs ending on or after 1 July 1999)

1. Unpaid CT (other than underpaid instalments)

Period of application	Rate %
From 6 September 2004	7.5
6 December 2003 to 5 September 2004	6.5
6 August 2003 to 5 December 2003	5.5
6 November 2001 to 5 August 2003	6.5
6 May 2001 to 5 November 2001	7.5
6 February 2000 to 5 May 2001	8.5
6 March 1999 to 5 February 2000	7.5
6 January 1999 to 5 March 1999	8.5

2. Underpaid instalments

Period of application	Rate %
From 16 August 2004	5.75
21 June 2004 to 15 August 2004	5.50
17 May 2004 to 20 June 2004	5.25
16 February 2004 to 16 May 2004	5.00
17 November 2003 to 15 February 2004	4.75

Period of application	Rate %
21 July 2003 to 16 November 2003	4.5
17 February 2003 to 20 July 2003	4.75
19 November 2001 to 16 February 2003	5.00
15 October 2001 to 18 November 2001	5.5
1 October 2001 to 14 October 2001	5.75
13 August 2001 to 30 September 2001	6.00
21 May 2001 to 12 August 2001	6.25
16 April 2001 to 20 May 2001	6.5
19 February 2001 to 15 April 2001	6.75
20 April 2000 to 18 February 2001	7.00
21 February 2000 to 19 April 2000	8.00
24 January 2000 to 20 February 2000	7.75
15 November 1999 to 23 January 2000	7.5
20 September 1999 to 14 November 1999	7.25
21 June 1999 to 19 September 1999	7.00
19 April 1999 to 20 June 1999	7.25
15 February 1999 to 18 April 1999	7.5
18 January 1999 to 14 February 1999	8.00

Pre-CTSA

Period of application	Rate % pre-Pay and File	Rate % post-Pay and File
From 6 September 2004	5.75	6
6 December 2003 to 5 September 2004	5	5
6 August 2003 to 5 December 2003	4.25	4.25
6 November 2001 to 5 August 2003	5	5
6 May 2001 to 5 November 2001	5.75	6
6 February 2000 to 5 May 2001	6.5	6.75

Period of application	Rate % pre-Pay and File	Rate % post-Pay and File
6 March 1999 to 5 February 2000	5.75	5.75
6 January 1999 to 5 March 1999	6.5	6.5
6 August 1997 to 5 January 1999	7.25	7.5
6 February 1997 to 5 August 1997	6.25	6.25

Rates of interest on tax repayments

Rates of interest on overpaid corporation tax

With effect for **interest** periods commencing on 6 February 1997, the rates of interest for the purposes of overpaid corporation tax are different from those for other taxes. The rate of interest on overpaid corporation tax will depend on the accounting period for which the tax is due and, under self assessment, the nature of the tax repayable:

Self assessment

For accounting periods within the self assessment regime (CTSA) i.e. APs on or after 1 July 1999, the rates of interest on repayments of overpaid corporation tax are distinct from those for pre-CTSA periods, because the interest is taxable (see below).

In addition, there are separate provisions for:

- overpaid instalments of corporation tax; and
- payments of corporation tax made after the normal due date.

Pay and File and earlier periods

For accounting periods within Pay and File (APs ending after 30 September 1993) and accounting periods before Pay and File, interest on overpaid corporation tax, repayments of income tax and payments of tax credits in respect of franked investment income received is given at the appropriate rate shown in the relevant table below.

CTSA (APs ending on or after 1 July 1999)

1. Overpaid CT (other than overpaid instalments and early payments of CT not due by instalments)

Period of application	Rate %
From 6 September 2004	4
6 December 2003 to 5 September 2004	3
6 August 2003 to 5 December 2003	2
6 November 2001 to 5 August 2003	3

Period of application	Rate %
6 May 2001 to 5 November 2001	4
6 February 2000 to 5 May 2001	5
6 March 1999 to 5 February 2000	4
6 January 1999 to 5 March 1999	5

2. Overpaid instalments and early payments of CT not due by instalments

Period of application	Rate %
From 16 August 2004	4.50
21 June 2004 to 15 August 2004	4.25
17 May 2004 to 20 June 2004	4.00
16 February 2004 to 16 May 2004	3.75
17 November 2003 to 15 February 2004	3.5
21 July 2003 to 16 November 2003	3.25
17 February 2003 to 20 July 2003	3.50
19 November 2001 to 16 February 2003	3.75
15 October 2001 to 18 November 2001	4.25
1 October 2001 to 14 October 2001	4.50
13 August 2001 to 30 September 2001	4.75
21 May 2001 to 12 August 2001	5.00
16 April 2001 to 20 May 2001	5.25
19 February 2001 to 15 April 2001	5.5
21 February 2000 to 18 February 2001	5.75
24 January 2000 to 20 February 2000	5.5
15 November 1999 to 23 January 2000	5.25
20 September 1999 to 14 November 1999	5.00
21 June 1999 to 19 September 1999	4.75
19 April 1999 to 20 June 1999	5.00

Period of application	Rate %
15 February 1999 to 18 April 1999	5.25
18 January 1999 to 14 February 1999	5.75

Pay and File

Period of application	Rate %
From 6 September 2004	2.75
6 December 2003 to 5 September 2004	2
6 August 2003 to 5 December 2003	1.25
6 November 2001 to 5 August 2003	2
6 May 2001 to 5 November 2001	2.75
6 February 2000 to 5 May 2001	3.5
6 March 1999 to 5 February 2000	2.75
6 January 1999 to 5 March 1999	3.25
6 August 1997 to 5 January 1999	4
6 February 1996 to 5 August 1997	3.25
6 March 1995 to 5 February 1996	4
6 October 1994 to 5 March 1995	3.25
6 January 1994 to 5 October 1994	2.5
1 October 1993 to 5 January 1994	3.25

Pre-Pay and File

Period of application	Rate %
From 6 September 2004	5.75
6 December 2003 to 5 September 2004	5
6 August 2003 to 5 December 2003	4.25
6 November 2001 to 5 August 2003	5
6 May 2001 to 5 November 2001	5.75
6 February 2000 to 5 May 2001	6.5
6 March 1999 to 5 February 2000	5.75

Period of application	Rate %
6 January 1999 to 5 March 1999	6.5
6 August 1997 to 5 January 1999	7.25
6 February 1996 to 5 August 1997	6.25

Time limits for elections and claims

In the absence of any provision to the contrary, the normal rule is that claims are to be made within six years from the end of the relevant chargeable period for accounting periods within self-assessment.

In certain cases the Board *may* permit an extension of the strict time limit in relation to certain elections and claims.

Provision	Time limit	References
Stock transferred to a connected party on cessation of trade to be valued at higher cost or sale price	2 years from end of accounting period in which trade ceased	ICTA 1988, s. 100(1C)
Carry-back of ACT (from accounting periods beginning *before* 6 April 1999 only)	2 years from end of accounting period	Former ICTA 1988, s. 239(3)
Surrender of ACT (from accounting periods beginning *before* 6 April 1999 only)	6 years from end of surrendering company's accounting period	Former ICTA 1988, s. 240(1), (6)
Carry-forward of trading losses	Relief is given automatically	ICTA 1988, s. 393(1)
Set-off of trading losses against profits of the same, or an earlier, accounting period	2 years from end of accounting period in which loss incurred	ICTA 1988, s. 393A(1), (10)
Group relief • where claimant company's accounting period is under self-assessment	Claims to group relief must be made (or withdrawn) by the later of: (1) 12 months after the claimant company's filing date for the return for the accounting period covered by the claim; (2) 30 days after a closure notice is issued on the completion of an enquiry; (3) 30 days after the Revenue issue a notice of amendment to a return following the completion of an enquiry (issued where the company fails to amend the return itself); or (4) 30 days after the determination of any appeal against a Revenue amendment (as in (3) above).	ICTA 1988, s. 412 and FA 1998, Sch. 18, para. 74

Provision	Time limit	References
	'Enquiry' in the above does not include a restricted enquiry into an amendment to a return (restricted because the time limit for making an enquiry into the return itself has expired), where the amendment consists of a group relief claim or withdrawal of claim. These time limits have priority over any other general time limits for amending returns and are subject to the Revenue permitting an extension to the time limits.	
• where claimant company's accounting period is under Pay and File	6 years from end of claimant company's accounting period (or such longer time as the Revenue permit subject to a maximum extension of 3 months) although a claim can only be made within 2 years of the end of the accounting period where an assessment has become final	ICTA 1988, s. 412, and former Sch. 17A, para. 2
Set-off of loss on disposal of shares in unquoted trading company against income of investment company	2 years from end of accounting period	ICTA 1988, s. 573(2)
Surrender of company tax refund within group	Before refund made to surrendering company	FA 1989, s. 102(2)
Election for deemed transfer of capital asset to another group company prior to disposal to third party	2 years from end of accounting period of actual vendor in which it's disposal to third party made	TCGA 1992, s. 171A
Notification of expenditure on plant and machinery on which capital allowances to be claimed[1]	2 years from end of accounting period to which claim relates	Former FA 1994, s. 118(3)
Relief for a non-trading deficit on loan relationships (including any non-trading exchange losses)	2 years from end of period in which deficit arises, or, in the case of a claim to carry forward the deficit, 2 years from end of the accounting period following the deficit period, or within such further period as the Board may allow	FA 1996, s. 83(6), (7)
General claim to capital allowances under self assessment	Claims to capital allowances must be made (or amended or withdrawn) by the later of: (1) 12 months after the claimant company's filing date for the return for the accounting period covered by the claim; (2) 30 days after a closure notice is issued on the completion of an enquiry; (3) 30 days after the Revenue issue a notice of amendment to a return following the completion of an enquiry (issued where the company fails to amend the return itself); or (4) 30 days after the determination of any appeal against a Revenue amendment (as in (3) above).	FA 1998, Sch. 18, para. 82

Provision	Time limit	References
	'Enquiry' in the above does not include a restricted enquiry into an amendment to a return (restricted because the time limit for making an enquiry into the return itself has expired), where the amendment consists of a group relief claim or withdrawal of a claim. These time limits have priority over any other general time limits for amending returns and are subject to the Revenue permitting an extension to the time limits.	
Certain plant and machinery treated as 'short life' assets	2 years from end of period chargeable/ basis period	CAA 2001, s. 85
Set-off of capital allowances on special leasing	2 years from end of accounting period	CAA 2001, s. 260(3), (6)
Transfer between connected parties of certain assets, eligible for capital allowances, at tax-written down value	2 years from date of sale	CAA 2001, s. 569(1)

Note

[1] Requirement to notify abolished by Finance Act 2000 with effect for claims where the time limit falls after 31 March 2000.

GENERAL

Capital allowances: rates

Plant and machinery allowances

A: First-year allowances (FYAs) and writing-down allowances (WDAs)

Nature of expenditure[1]	Type of business eligible to claim FYAs and WDAs[6]	Date expenditure incurred	FYA rate p.a.	WDA rate p.a.
Expenditure on plant and machinery[2]	Non-SMEs	On or after 1 July 1998	Nil	25%
Expenditure on plant and machinery for use primarily in Northern Ireland (CAA 2001, s. 40ff.)	SMEs	On or after 12 May 1998 and on or before 11 May 2002	100%	25%
Expenditure on plant and machinery[3] (CAA 2001, s. 44)	SEs subject to corporation tax	On or after 1 April 2004 and on or before 31 March 2005	50%	25%
	SEs subject to income tax	On or after 6 April 2004 and on or before 5 April 2005	50%	25%
	MEs subject to corporation tax	On or after 1 April 2004	40%	25%
	MEs subject to income tax	On or after 6 April 2004	40%	25%
	SMEs subject to corporation tax	On or after 1 July 1998 and on or before 31 March 2004	40%	25%
	SMEs subject to income tax	On or after 1 July 1998 and on or before 5 April 2004	40%	25%

Nature of expenditure[1]	Type of business eligible to claim FYAs and WDAs[6]	Date expenditure incurred	FYA rate p.a.	WDA rate p.a.
Expenditure on information and communications technology (CAA 2001, s. 45)	SEs	On or after 1 April 2000 and on or before 31 March 2004	100%	25%
Expenditure on new energy-saving plant or machinery (CAA 2001, s. 45A–45C)	Any	On or after 1 April 2001	100%	25%
Expenditure on cars with low carbon dioxide emissions (CAA 2001, s. 45D)	Any	On or after 17 April 2002 and on or before 31 March 2008	100%	25%
Expenditure on plant or machinery for gas refuelling station (CAA 2001, s. 45E)	Any	On or after 17 April 2002 and on or before 31 March 2008	100%	25%
Expenditure on plant and machinery for use wholly in a ring fence trade which is long-life asset expenditure	Company	On or after 17 April 2002	24%	6%
Expenditure on plant and machinery for use wholly in a ring fence trade other than long-life asset expenditure	Company	On or after 17 April 2002	100%	25%
Expenditure on new environmentally beneficial plant or machinery (CAA 2001, s. 45H–45J)	Any	On or after 1 April 2003	100%	25%
Expenditure on car above cost threshold of £12,000[4] (CAA 2001, s. 74ff.)	Any	On or after 11 March 1992	Nil	lower of: 25% and £3,000

Nature of expenditure[1]	Type of business eligible to claim FYAs and WDAs[6]	Date expenditure incurred	FYA rate p.a.	WDA rate p.a.
Long-life asset expenditure[5] (CAA 2001, s. 90ff.)	Any	On or after 26 November 1996, or on or after 1 January 2001 if in pursuance of contract entered into before 26 November 1996	Nil	6%

Notes

[1] There are single asset pools, class pools and the main pool (CAA 2001, s. 54(1)).

(a)   Qualifying expenditure on the following is allocated to separate single asset pools (CAA 2001, s. 54(3)) –

- car above the cost threshold (CAA 2001, s. 74ff.): cost threshold is £12,000: writing-down allowance is 25% p.a. on reducing balance basis but cannot exceed £3,000 (i.e., 25% × £12,000 p.a.);
- short-life asset (CAA 2001, s. 83ff.): irrevocable election required to be made;
- ship (CAA 2001, s. 127ff.): special rules apply for postponement of first-year and writing-down allowances;
- plant or machinery provided or used partly for purposes other than those of qualifying activity (CAA 2001, s. 205ff.);
- plant or machinery for which a partial depreciation subsidy has been received (CAA 2001, s. 209ff.); and
- to the extent of the contribution, plant and machinery for which a contribution has been made (CAA 2001, s. 537ff.).

(b)   Qualifying expenditure on the following is allocated to a class pool (CAA 2001, s. 54(5)) –

- long-life assets (CAA 2001, s. 90ff.); and
- plant or machinery used for overseas leasing which is not protected leasing (CAA 2001, s. 105ff.): first-year allowance is nil, and writing down allowance is 10% p.a. (instead of 25% p.a.).

(c)   Qualifying expenditure may be allocated to the main pool if it is not to be allocated to a single asset or class pool.

[2] Expenditure on plant and machinery other than expenditure listed below within this Table.

[3] Excludes long-life asset expenditure.

[4] Car with cost above the cost threshold is also known as an expensive car.

Before 11 March 1992, the cost threshold was £8,000 and writing-down allowance was lower of: (a) 25%, and (b) £2,000 (i.e. 25% × £8,000 p.a.).

Expenditure on car that does not exceed cost threshold of £12,000 (inexpensive car) is allocated to the main pool (CAA 2001, s. 54(6)).

Expenditure on car that does not exceed cost threshold used to be allocated to a class pool (inexpensive car pool) for –

- companies: accounting periods preceding accounting period that includes (a) 1 April 2000, or (b) 1 April 2001 if option of one year postponement chosen.
- others: periods of account preceding period of account that includes (a) 6 April 2000, or 6 April 2001 if option of one year postponement chosen.

[5] Long-life asset expenditure excludes expenditure on:

(a)   certain fixtures (CAA 2001, s. 93),

(b)   certain ships incurred before 1 January 2011 (CAA 2001, s. 94),

(c)   railway assets incurred before 1 January 2011 (CAA 2001, s. 95),

(d)   cars (CAA 2001, s. 96), and

(e)   expenditure within the annual relevant monetary limit of £100,000 (CAA 2001, s. 97–100).

[6] SMEs are small or medium-sized enterprises and SEs are small enterprises (CAA 2001, s. 47 and s. 48): see Table B below.

B: Small and medium-sized enterprises (CAA 2001, s. 47, 49)

A company or business is a *small enterprise* if:

- it qualifies (or is treated as qualifying) as small under the *Companies Act* 1985, s. 247, for the financial year of the company in which the expenditure is incurred; and

- it is not a member of a medium or large group (*Companies Act* 1985, s. 249) at the time the expenditure is incurred.

A company or business is a *small or medium-sized enterprise* if:

- it qualifies (or is treated as qualifying) as small or medium-sized under the *Companies Act* 1985, s. 247, for the financial year of the company in which the expenditure is incurred; and

- it is not a member of a large group (*Companies Act* 1985, s. 249) at the time the expenditure is incurred.

Under the *Companies Act* 1985, s. 247, a company qualifies as small or medium-sized for a financial year if two or more of the requirements shown below are met in that and the preceding financial year. A group is small or medium-sized under the *Companies Act* 1985, s. 249 in a year in which it satisfies two or more of the requirements per relevant category, as shown in the tables below.

There are two tables set out below. The first table is in respect of years ending on or after 30 January 2004 (but see exception below) and takes into account the changes made by the *Companies Act 1985 (Accounts of Small and Medium-Sized Enterprises and Audit Exemption) (Amendment) Regulations* 2004 (SI 2004/16). The second table is in respect of years ending before 30 January 2004. However, as an exception, the second table applies also to a financial year that only ends on or after 30 January 2004 by reason of an exercise of the power (conferred by the *Companies Act* 1985, s. 225) to alter the accounting reference date, by the giving of a notice (namely, Form 225, *Change of accounting reference date*) to the Registrar of Companies on or after 9 January 2004.

The first table is as follows:

Type of company	Requirements	
Small company	Turnover	Not more than £5.6m
	Balance sheet total	Not more than £2.8m
	Number of employees	Not more than 50

Type of company	Requirements	
Medium-sized company	Turnover	Not more than £22.8m
	Balance sheet total	Not more than £11.4m
	Number of employees	Not more than 250
Small group	Aggregate turnover	Not more than £5.6m net (or £6.72m gross)
	Aggregate balance sheet total	Not more than £2.8m net (or £3.36m gross)
	Aggregate number of employees	Not more than 50
Medium-sized group	Aggregate turnover	Not more than £22.8m net (or £27.36m gross)
	Aggregate balance sheet total	Not more than £11.4m net (or £13.68m gross)
	Aggregate number of employees	Not more than 250

The second table is as follows:

Type of company	Requirements	
Small company	Turnover	Not more than £2.8m
	Balance sheet total	Not more than £1.4m
	Number of employees	Not more than 50
Medium-sized company	Turnover	Not more than £11.2m
	Balance sheet total	Not more than £5.6m
	Number of employees	Not more than 250
Small group	Aggregate turnover	Not more than £2.8m net (or £3.6m gross)
	Aggregate balance sheet total	Not more than £1.4m net (or £1.68m gross)
	Aggregate number of employees	Not more than 50

Type of company	Requirements	
Medium-sized group	Aggregate turnover	Not more than £11.2m net (or £13.44m gross)
	Aggregate balance sheet total	Not more than £5.6m net (or £6.72m gross)
	Aggregate number of employees	Not more than 250

Industrial buildings;[1] hotels and sports pavilions;[2] and agricultural buildings and structures[3]

Date expenditure incurred	Initial allowance	Writing down allowance
On or after 1 November 1993	Nil	4%
1 November 1992–31 October 1993	20%	4%
1 April 1986–31 October 1992	Nil	4%

Notes
[1] The non-industrial element of an industrial building will qualify for allowances provided it does not exceed 25%.
[2] A qualifying hotel must provide standard hotel facilities, have at least 10 letting bedrooms and be open for at least four months between April-October, inclusive (CAA 2001, s. 279).
[3] Includes expenditure on farmhouses and buildings, cottages, fences and other works incurred for the purposes of husbandry on agricultural land (a maximum of $1/3$ of expenditure on farmhouses may qualify) (CAA 2001, s. 369).

Enterprise Zones:[1] Industrial Buildings; Hotels and Commercial Buildings or structures[2]

Date expenditure incurred	Initial allowance	Writing down allowance
Contract to be made within 10 years of site being included within the enterprise zone (but not expenditure incurred over 20 years after the date of the site being included)	100%	25%

Notes
[1] Areas designated by Orders made under the *Local Government, Planning and Land Act* 1980 or equivalent Northern Ireland legislation (CAA 2001, s. 298(3)).
[2] Buildings or structures used for the purposes of a trade, profession or vocation (but not an industrial building or qualifying hotel) or used as offices; but not a dwelling house (CAA 2001, s. 281).

Renovation of business premises in disadvantaged areas (CAA 2001, s. 360Aff.)

Date expenditure incurred	Initial allowance	Writing down allowance
On or after such day as the Treasury may by order appoint.[1]	100%	25%

Date not announced at time of going to press.

Flat conversion allowances (CAA 2001, s. 393Aff.)[1]

Date expenditure incurred	Initial allowance	Writing down allowance
On or after 11 May 2001	100%	25%

Note
[1] Expenditure on renovating or converting space above shops and other commercial premises.

Dredging allowances (CAA 2001, s. 484ff.)

Date expenditure incurred	Initial allowance	Writing down allowance
On or after 1 April 1986	Nil	4%

Mineral extraction allowances[1] (CAA 2001, s. 394ff.)

Date expenditure incurred	Initial allowance	Writing down allowance
On or after 1 April 1986	Nil	25%[2]

Notes
[1] Includes mines, oil wells and geothermal energy sources.
[2] Certain expenditure, on the acquisition of a mineral deposit and/or rights over such a deposit, qualifies for a 10% WDA.

Research and development allowances[1] (CAA 2001, s. 437ff.)

Date expenditure incurred	Initial allowance	Writing down allowance
On or after 5 November 1962	100%	No provision for WDAs

Notes
[1] Covers expenditure incurred for carrying out research and development, or providing facilities for such research, but not that incurred on the acquisition of rights in, or arising out of, research and development.

Patent allowances[1] (CAA 2001, s. 464ff.)

Date expenditure incurred	Initial allowance	Writing down allowance
On or after 1 April 1986	Nil	25%

Notes
[1] The purchase of patent rights includes the acquisition of a licence in respect of a patent.

Know-how allowances[1] (CAA 2001, s. 452)

Date expenditure incurred	Initial allowance	Writing down allowance
On or after 1 April 1986	Nil	25%

Notes
[1] 'Know-how' means any industrial information and techniques likely to assist in: (i) the manufacture or processing of goods or materials; (ii) all aspects of working a mine, oil well or mineral deposit; (iii) carrying out agricultural, forestry or fishing operations.

Assured tenancy allowances (CAA 2001, s. 490)

Date expenditure incurred	Initial allowance	Writing down allowance
1 April 1986–31 March 1992	Nil	4%

Enterprise zones

Enterprise zones have been designated as follows:

Statutory instrument	Area	Start date
1981/309	Belfast	21 October 1981
1981/757	Lower Swansea Valley	11 June 1981
1981/764	Corby	22 June 1981
1981/852	Dudley	10 July 1981
1981/950	Wakefield (Langthwaite Grange)	31 July 1981
1981/975	Clydebank	3 August 1981
1981/1024	Salford	12 August 1981
1981/1025	Trafford Park	12 August 1981
1981/1069	Glasgow	18 August 1981
1981/1070	Gateshead	25 August 1981
1981/1071	Newcastle	25 August 1981
1981/1072	Speke	25 August 1981
1981/1378	Hartlepool	23 October 1981
1982/462	Isle of Dogs	26 April 1982
1983/226	Londonderry	13 September 1983
1983/896	Delyn and Flint	21 July 1983
1983/907	Wellingborough	26 July 1983
1983/1007	Rotherham	16 August 1983
1983/1304	Scunthorpe (excluding Glanford)	23 September 1983
1983/1305	Wakefield (extended to Dale Lane and Kinsley)	23 September 1983
1983/1331	Workington (Allerdale)	4 October 1983
1983/1359	Invergordon	7 October 1983
1983/1452	North-West Kent (Gillingham and Gravesend)	31 October 1983
1983/1473	Middlesbrough (Britannia)	8 November 1983
1983/1639	North-East Lancashire (Burnley, Hyndburn, Pendle and Rossendale)	7 December 1983
1983/1816	Arbroath	9 January 1984
1983/1817	Dundee	9 January 1984
1983/1852	Telford	13 January 1984
1984/347	Glanford (Flixborough)	13 April 1984
1984/443–444	Milford Haven Waterway	24 April 1984
1984/1403	Dudley (extended to Round Oak)	3 October 1984
1985/137	Lower Swansea Valley (extended)	6 March 1985
1986/1557	North-West Kent (extended to Chatham and Rochester-upon-Medway)	10 October 1986
1989/145	Inverclyde	3 March 1989
1989/794	Sunderland (Castletown and Doxford Park)	27 April 1990
1989/795	Sunderland (Hylton Riverside and Southwick)	27 April 1990
1993/23	Lanarkshire (Hamilton)	1 February 1993
1993/24	Lanarkshire (Motherwell)	1 February 1993
1993/25	Lanarkshire (Monklands)	1 February 1993
1995/2624	Dearne Valley (Barnsley, Doncaster, Rotherham)	3 November 1995
1995/2625	Holmewood (North East Derbyshire)	3 November 1995
1995/2738	Bassetlaw	16 November 1995
1995/2758	Ashfield	21 November 1995
1995/2812	East Durham (No. 1 to No. 6)	29 November 1995
1996/106	Tyne Riverside (North Tyneside)	19 February 1996
1996/1981	Tyne Riverside (Silverlink North Scheme)	26 August 1996
1996/1981	Tyne Riverside (Silverlink Business Park Scheme)	26 August 1996

Statutory instrument	Area	Start date
1996/1981	Tyne Riverside (Middle Engine Lane Scheme)	26 August 1996
1996/1981	Tyne Riverside (New York Industrial Park Scheme)	26 August 1996
1996/1981	Tyne Riverside (Balliol Business Park West Scheme)	26 August 1996
1996/2435	Tyne Riverside (Baltic Enterprise Park Scheme)	21 October 1996
1996/2435	Tyne Riverside (Viking Industrial Park – Wagonway West Scheme)	21 October 1996
1996/2435	Tyne Riverside (Viking Industrial Park – Blackett Street Scheme)	21 October 1996
1996/2435	Tyne Riverside (Viking Industrial Park – Western Road Scheme)	21 October 1996

Note
Enterprise zones last for ten years from the start date.

Expensive cars: restriction on hire charge

(ICTA 1988, s. 578A; ITTOIA 2005, s. 50)

Restriction applies to the hiring of a car where the retail price when new exceeds £12,000. There is a permanent disallowance of part of the hire cost. The allowable proportion is calculated as: $\frac{(£12,000 + P)}{2P}$ where P is the retail price of the car when new. So a car with a monthly hire cost of £320 and a retail price of £16,000 will have a permanent restriction of £40 per month as the allowable amount is £320 x $\frac{(£12,000 + £16,000)}{£32,000}$.

NB the restriction applies only to the hire cost. If the monthly payment includes, for example, a maintenance cost then the restriction does not apply to that part.

Community investment relief

Tax relief is claimed on an annual basis, at the rate of five per cent of the 'invested amount' for the tax year (or accounting period for a corporate investor) in which the investment date falls and the four subsequent tax years (or accounting periods). If the investment is by way of a loan, the 'invested amount' is not necessarily the amount of the loan made available at the beginning of the five-year investment period. The tax relief cannot reduce the taxpayer's tax liability below zero for any single tax year (or accounting period) (FA 2002, Sch. 16, para. 19 and 20).

Gifts of assets

Nature of asset	Date(s) of relief	Effect of relief
Plant or machinery used by, or stock manufactured or sold by a trader that is given to a charity, etc. (ICTA 1988, s. 83A)	From 27 July 1999	No disposal value brought into account as trading receipt or for capital allowances purposes

Nature of asset	Date(s) of relief	Effect of relief
Listed shares and securities, unlisted shares and securities that are dealt in on recognised stock exchanges, units in unit trusts, etc. given to a charity by an individual or company (ICTA 1988, s. 587B)	From April 2000	The full value of the gift is deductible when computing profits for IT or CT purposes
Property settled by gift on a UK-resident trust which has a charity as beneficiary and the settlor retains an interest (FA 2000, s. 44)	From April 2000	The trust income allocated to the settlor under ICTA 1988, Pt. XV will be reduced by an amount equal to the income paid to the charity in the year

Note

[1] Countries are designated by Treasury Order and include those in Appendix 5 to the World Bank's 1997 Annual report (as revised from time to time) as eligible for certain funding. FA 1998, s. 47 was repealed by FA 1999, s. 55 which introduced relief under ICTA 1988, s. 83A.

Due dates

Income tax and capital gains tax 2005–06

Tax is paid on 31 January next following the year of assessment as a single sum covering capital gains tax and income tax on all sources. Interim payments on account may be required. No interim payments are required for a year of assessment if the tax paid by assessment for the preceding year was less than £500 or 20% of the total tax liability for that year. These will normally be half the amount of the net tax payable for the preceding year, but may be reduced to half the current year's liability, if less. Net tax is previous year's tax after taking off tax deducted at source and tax on dividends. For 2005–06, the following due dates apply:

First interim payment 31 January 2006
Second interim payment 31 July 2006
Final balancing payment 31 January 2007

Note

If a return is not issued until after 31 October 2005 and the tax payer has notified chargeability by 5 October 2005, the due date for the final payment becomes three months from the issue of the return (TMA 1970, s. 59B).

Interest and surcharges

Income tax and capital gains tax 2005–06

Interest (TMA 1970, s. 86)

Interest is payable from the 'relevant date':

Payment	Relevant date
First interim payment[1]	31 January 2006
Second interim payment	31 July 2006

Final payment	31 January 2007
Tax due on an amendment to a return	31 January 2007
Tax due on determination of appeal	31 January 2007

Notes
(1) Where the taxpayer has provided the Revenue in good time with the information required to issue a statement of account ahead of the payment date of 31 January, but no statement is received before 1 January, interest on the tax to be paid will run from 30 days after the taxpayer is actually notified rather than from 31 January.
(2) Where notice to make a return is issued after 31 October 2005, then, provided there has been no failure to notify chargeability under TMA 1970, s. 7, the relevant date becomes the last day in the period of three months beginning with the day notice to make a return was given.

Surcharges (TMA 1970, s. 59C)

Surcharges arise as follows:

Tax overdue	Surcharge
28 days	5% of tax overdue
6 months	further 5% of tax overdue

Note
Tax is not subject to a surcharge if it is taken into account for penalties for failure to notify – return over 12 months late or incorrect return. A surcharge will be repaid if one of these penalties is subsequently levied.

Surcharges apply to:

* final tax payments on self-assessments (this includes any amounts due as interim payments which remain unpaid);
* tax on inspector's amendments to a self-assessment made during or as a result of an audit; and
* discovery assessments.

Rates of interest on overdue income tax, capital gains tax and National Insurance contributions

The following tables give the rates of interest applicable under FA 1989, s. 178 and prescribed rates of interest (VATA 1994, s. 74 and former TMA 1970, s. 89).

Period of application	Rate %
From 6 September 2004	7.5
From 6 December 2003 to 5 September 2004	6.5
From 6 August 2003 to 5 December 2003	5.5
From 6 November 2001 to 5 August 2003	6.5
From 6 May 2001 to 5 November 2001	7.5
From 6 February 2000 to 5 May 2001	8.5
From 6 March 1999 to 5 February 2000	7.5
From 6 January 1999 to 5 March 1999	8.5
From 6 August 1997 to 5 January 1999	9.5
From 6 February 1997 to 5 August 1997	8.5

Note
(1) Fixed by Treasury order under SI 1989/1297.

Rates of interest on income tax, capital gains tax and National Insurance contributions repayments

Interest on tax repayments qualifying for repayment supplement, except for repayments made under the Pay and File regime, is given at the following rates:

Period of application	Rate %
From 6 September 2004	3.5
From 6 December 2003 to 5 September 2004	2.5
From 6 August 2003 to 5 December 2003	1.75
From 6 November 2001 to 5 August 2003	2.5
From 6 May 2001 to 5 November 2001	3.5
From 6 February 2000 to 5 May 2001	4
From 6 March 1999 to 5 February 2000	3
From 6 January 1999 to 5 March 1999	4
From 6 August 1997 to 5 January 1999	4.75
From 6 February 1997 to 5 August 1997	4

Note

The qualifying period is as set out below:

From the date of payment (deemed to be 31 January following the tax year in respect of tax deducted at source) to the date on which the order for the repayment is issued.

For periods to self-assessment, the qualifying period was:

Later of:

(i)   due date; or

(ii)   actual date of payment,

until the end of the tax month in which the repayment order was issued.

Interest rates on certificates of tax deposit (CTD)

Certificates of tax deposit (CTDs)

The interest rates that follow apply to CTDs issued under the Series 7 prospectus.

CTDs (Series 7) can be purchased to settle most tax liabilities, except PAYE, VAT and corporation tax falling due under Pay and File, or for subsequent encashment. (No CTDs are available for purchase for use against corporation tax liabilities since the start of the Pay and File regime.) A higher rate of interest is paid if the CTD is used in payment of tax. Interest is allowed/paid gross and is taxable.

Rates of interest vary according to the period for which the deposit is held. The rates in force at issue apply for one year; thereafter the rate applicable is that on the most recent anniversary of the date of issue.

Deposits must be maintained at £2,000 or over. A deposit of less than £100,000 can be made at any tax collection office. Larger deposits must be sent to the Bank of England (Drawing Office) (for the General Account of the Commissioners of Inland Revenue, No. 23411007) with a confirmatory letter to the Inland Revenue, Revenue Finance (CTD), Room B2, South Block, Barrington Road, Worthing, West Sussex BN12 4XH.

Copies of the Series 7 prospectus, giving full details concerning CTDs, can be obtained from any collection office or the Central Accounting Office.

Rates applicable over recent years have been as follows:

Certificates of tax deposit (Series 7): rates of interest

Deposits on or after	Deposits under £100,000		Deposits of £100,000 or more									
			Deposits held for under 1 month		Deposits held for 1 to under 3 months		Deposits held for 3 to under six months		Deposits held for 6 to under 9 months		Deposits held for 9–12 months	
	Applied in payment of tax %	Cash value %	Applied in payment of tax %	Cash value %	Applied in payment of tax %	Cash value %	Applied in payment of tax %	Cash value %	Applied in payment of tax %	Cash value %	Applied in payment of tax %	Cash value %
7 May 1997	2.75	1.50	2.75	1.50	5.50	2.75	5.25	2.75	5.50	2.75	5.25	2.75
9 June 1997	3	1.50	3	1.50	5.50	2.75	5.50	2.75	5.50	2.75	5.50	2.75
11 July 1997	3.25	1.75	3.25	1.75	6	3	5.75	3	5.75	3	6	3
8 Aug. 1997	4.50	2.25	4.50	2.25	6	3	6	3	6	3	5.75	3
7 Nov. 1997	4	2	4	2	6.50	3.25	6.50	3.25	6.25	3.25	6.25	3.25
5 June 1998	4	2	4	2	6.50	3.25	6.25	3.25	6.25	3.25	6	3
9 Oct. 1998	3.75	2	3.75	2	6.25	3.25	5.75	3	5.50	2.75	5.25	2.75
6 Nov. 1998	3.25	1.75	3.25	1.75	5.75	3	5.25	2.75	5	2.50	4.75	2.50
11 Dec. 1998	3.25	1.75	3	1.50	5.25	2.75	4.75	2.50	4.50	2.25	4.25	2.25
8 Jan. 1999	2.50	1.25	2.50	1.25	5	2.50	4.50	2.25	4	2	4	2
5 Feb. 1999	1.75	1	1.75	1	4.50	2.25	4	2	3.75	2	3.75	2
9 Apr. 1999	1.75	1	1.75	1	4.50	2	4	2	3.75	2	3.75	2
11 June 1999	1.50	.75	1.50	.75	4	2	4	2	4	2	4	2
9 Sept. 1999	1.75	1	1.75	1	4.50	2.25	4.50	2.25	4.50	2.25	4.50	2.25
4 Nov. 1999	2	1	2	1	5	2.50	4.75	2.50	4.75	2.50	4.75	2.50
14 Jan. 2000	2.25	1.25	2.25	1.25	5	2.50	5	2.50	5	2.50	5.25	2.75
11 Feb. 2000	2.50	1.25	2.50	1.25	5.25	2.50	5	2.50	5.25	2.75	5.25	2.75
9 Feb. 2001	2.25	1.25	2.25	1.25	4.75	2.25	4.25	2.25	4.25	2.25	4	2
6 Apr. 2001	2	1	2	1	4.25	2	4	2	3.75	2	3.50	1.75
11 May 2001	2	1	2	1	4	2	4	2	3.75	2	3.75	2
3 Aug. 2001	1.50	.75	1.50	.75	4	2	3.75	1.875	3.75	1.875	3.75	1.875
5 Oct. 2001	1	.50	1	.50	3.25	1.75	3	1.50	3	1.50	3	1.50
9 Nov. 2001	.50	.25	.50	.25	2.75	1.50	2.50	1.25	2.25	1.25	2.25	1.25
7 Feb. 2003	.25	Nil	.25	Nil	2.75	1.25	2.25	1.00	2.25	1.00	2.00	1.00
11 July 2003	Nil	Nil	Nil	Nil	2.50	1.25	2.25	1.00	2.00	1.00	2.00	1.00
7 Nov. 2003	.25	Nil	.25	Nil	3.00	1.50	3.00	1.50	3.00	1.50	3.00	1.50
6 Feb. 2004	.50	.25	.50	.25	3.00	1.50	3.00	1.50	3.00	1.50	3.00	1.50

Deposits on or after	Deposits under £100,000		Deposits of £100,000 or more									
			Deposits held for under 1 month		Deposits held for 1 to under 3 months		Deposits held for 3 to under six months		Deposits held for 6 to under 9 months		Deposits held for 9–12 months	
	Applied in payment of tax %	Cash value %	Applied in payment of tax %	Cash value %	Applied in payment of tax %	Cash value %	Applied in payment of tax %	Cash value %	Applied in payment of tax %	Cash value %	Applied in payment of tax %	Cash value %
7 May 2004	.75	.25	.75	.25	3.25	1.50	3.25	1.50	3.25	1.50	3.25	1.50
11 June 2004	1.00	.50	1.00	.50	3.75	1.75	3.50	1.75	3.75	1.75	3.75	1.75
6 Aug. 2004	1.25	.50	1.25	.50	3.75	1.75	3.50	1.75	3.75	1.75	3.75	1.75

Remission of tax for official error

(ESC A19)

Under ESC A19, arrears of income tax and capital gains tax may be given up if they result from the Revenue's failure to make proper and timely use of information supplied by the taxpayer, or in certain circumstances by the taxpayer's employer or the Department for Work and Pensions.

The taxpayer must have reasonably believed that his or her affairs were in order. Tax will normally only be given up where there was a gap of 12 months or more between the Revenue receiving the information that tax was due, and notifying the taxpayer of the arrears.

Revenue addresses and telephone numbers

The Inland Revenue website contains full details of contact addresses and numbers, including in particular the following:

- Helplines and orderlines: *http://www.inlandrevenue.gov.uk/menus/helpline.htm*
- All local Tax Offices, National Insurance Contribution Offices, and Valuation Offices:*http://www.inlandrevenue.gov.uk/local/index.htm*
- Specialist offices:*http://www.inlandrevenue.gov.uk/menus/officesmenu.htm*
- Inland Revenue enquiry centres: *http://www.inlandrevenue.gov.uk/enq/index.htm*
- Inland Revenue recovery offices: *http://www.inlandrevenue.gov.uk/local/recovery.htm*

Other useful internet addresses

Treasury Home Page

http://www.hm-treasury.gov.uk

Inland Revenue Home Page

http://www.inlandrevenue.gov.uk

Inland Revenue Self Assessment Pages

http://www.inlandrevenue.gov.uk/sa/index.htm

CCTA Government Information Service

http://www.open.gov.uk

HMSO – Statutory Instruments

http://www.hmso.gov.uk/stat.htm

For statutory instruments made by the National Assembly for Wales –

http://www.wales-legislation.hmso.gov.uk/legislation/wales/w-stat.htm

For statutory instruments made by the Scottish Parliament –
http://www.scotland-legislation.hmso.gov.uk/legislation/scotland/s-stat.htm

Also of interest are:

Government news releases

http://www.gnn.gov.uk and

http://www.coi.gov.uk/whatsnew/press/index.shtml

Inland Revenue news releases

http://www.inlandrevenue.gov.uk/news/press.htm

CIOT

http://www.tax.org.uk/html/PR/PR_index.htm

For press releases, select 'News'.

ICAEW Tax Faculty

http://www.icaew.co.uk

For news releases, select 'Press office' then 'News releases'.

Inland Revenue benefits in kind

http://www.inlandrevenue.gov.uk/biks/index.htm

SMMT – CO_2 emissions data

http://www.smmt.co.uk

Employers information

http://www.inlandrevenue.gov.uk/employers/index.htm

Inland Revenue Tax Credits

http://www.inlandrevenue.gov.uk/menus/credits.htm

Useful helplines

IR Charities (Bootle)

Telephone/form requests: (0845) 302 0203

IR Charities (Scotland)

Telephone/form requests: (0845) 302 0203

Gift Aid–

Telephone: (0845) 302 0203

E-mail: charities@inlandrevenue.gov.uk

Child Tax Credit

Open seven days 8:00am to 8:00pm.

Great Britain: Telephone: (0845) 300 3900

Northern Ireland: Telephone: (0845) 603 2000

Internet applications: Monday to Friday 8:00am to 10:00pm

Saturday and Sunday 10:00am to 6:00pm.

Construction Industry Scheme (CIS)

Orderline: (0845) 300 0551

Contractors Helpline: (0845) 733 5588

Sub-contractors Helpline: (0845) 300 0581

NI Services to Pensions Industry

Telephone: (0845) 915 0150

Corporation Tax Self Assessment Orderline

Telephone: (0845) 300 6555

E-mail: saorderline.ir@gtnet.gov.uk

Electronic Business

Telephone: (0845) 605 5999 (or (0845) 300 3938 for new tax credits)

E-mail: helpdesk@ir-efile.gov.uk

Employer's Orderline

Telephone: (0845) 764 6646

Employer's Helplines

For guidance on payroll matters including National Insurance contributions, PAYE, SSP, SMP and basic VAT registration.

New Employers:

Telephone: (0845) 607 0143

More experienced Employers:

Telephone: (0845) 714 3143

IHT general queries

Telephone (0845) 302 0900

Telephone: (0845) 234 1000 (Forms and Leaflets)

Individual Savings Accounts Helpline

Telephone: (0845) 604 1701

National Insurance: International Services Helpline

Telephone: (0845) 915 4811

From outside the UK

Dial international code then;

Telephone: 44 191 225 4811

National Minimum Wage
Helpline: (0845) 600 0678
Orderline: (0845) 845 0360
Northern Ireland open Monday to Friday 10:00am to 4:00pm
Telephone: (0845) 6500 207

Centre for Non-Residents Helplines
Non-resident Individuals Helpline:
Telephone: (0151) 472 6196
Non-resident Landlords Helpline:
Telephone: (0151) 472 6208/6209
Residence Status (Individuals):
Telephone: (0151) 472 6137
E-mail non-residents@inlandrevenue.gov.uk

Payment by Debit Card
For making Self Assessment payments by Debit Card (Switch, Solo, or Visa Delta).
Telephone: (0845) 305 1000

Self Assessment

Self Assessment Helpline
Telephone: (0845) 900 0444 (from abroad: +44 870 1555 445)

Class 2 NIC Helpline
Telephone: (0845) 915 4655

Self Assessment Orderline
Telephone: (0845) 900 0404
E-mail: saorderline.ir@gtnet.gov.uk
From abroad: Dial international access code, then;
Telephone: 44 870 1555 664

Shares Valuation: general queries
Nottingham
Helpline: (0115) 974 2222
Edinburgh
Helpline: (0131) 777 4000

Stakeholder pensions
Helpline: (0845) 601 2923

Stamp Office helpline
Helpline: (0845) 603 0135

Tax and Benefits Confidential Advice Line
Telephone: (0845) 608 6000

Taxation of Bank and Building Society Interest
Telephone: (0845) 077 6543

Trusts Helplines
Administration Period Helpline:
Telephone: (0131) 777 4030
Disaster Funds Helpline:
Telephone: (0151) 472 6061

Welsh Language
Telephone: (0845) 766 0830

Working Tax Credit
Great Britain: Telephone: (0845) 300 3900
Northern Ireland: Telephone: (0845) 603 2000

Useful addresses

Adjudicator

The Adjudicator's Office
Haymarket House
28 Haymarket
London SW1Y 4SP
Tel: (020) 7930 2292
Fax: (020) 7930 2298

IR Information Centre

(open to visitors)
Ground Floor
South West Wing
Bush House
Strand
London WC2B 4RD
Tel: (020) 7438 6420/6425

Parliamentary Ombudsman

Commissioner for administration
Millbank Tower
Millbank
London SW1P 4QP
Tel: (0845) 015 4033/(020) 7217 4160
Fax: (020) 7217 4000

Special Commissioners of Income Tax

15–19 Bedford Avenue
London WC1B 3AS
Tel: (020) 7631 4242
Fax: (020) 7436 4151

Clearance applications

Clearance Applications

The following information appears on the Inland Revenue's website at http://www.inlandrevenue.gov.uk/cap/index.htm#1.

Clearances and Approvals provided for in the Taxes Acts

The Taxes Acts say that advance clearance or approval may be given to some transactions. These are listed below together with the addresses to which you should send applications.

Booklet Code of Practice 10 tells you what other information and advice is available to you from the Inland Revenue.

Please read this before sending an application

Please do not fax an application that contains confidential information or a large number of pages without the prior agreement of the clearance section.

One Stop Shop for clearances

Contents

Clearance applications
- Capital gains
- Demergers
- Company purchase of own shares
- Transactions in securities
- Company migrations
- Transactions in shares or debentures
- Advance Pricing Agreements
- Controlled Foreign Companies
- Funding Issues
- Transactions in land
- Transfers of long term business between life assurance companies
- Corporate Venturing Scheme

Statutory approvals
- Employee share schemes
- Pensions
- Qualifying Life Assurance Polices

Clearance applications
Capital gains

Under s. 138, TCGA 1992:

Share exchanges, company reconstructions or amalgamations.

Under s. 139, TCGA 1992:

Company reconstructions or amalgamations involving a transfer of business.

Under s. 140B, TCGA 1992:

Transfer of UK trade between companies resident in different European Union Member States.

Under s. 140D, TCGA 1992:

Transfer of non-UK trade by UK company resident in different European Union Member State.

Please send applications for clearance to:

William Perrett
Revenue Policy, Capital and Savings
Capital Gains Clearance Section
Sapphire House
550 Streetsbrook Road
Solihull
West Midlands B91 1QU

Company migrations

Notices to be given under s. 130, FA 1988.

Notification of company migration and approval of arrangements for payment of tax liabilities, s. 130, FA 1988: (see Statement of Practice 2/90).

Please send applications for clearance to:

Mark Ritchie
Revenue Policy, International
Business Tax Group (Company Migrations)
Victory House
30–34 Kingsway
London WC2B 6ES

Transactions in Shares or Debentures

Under s. 765 & s. 765A, ICTA 1988:

Applications for treasury consent under s. 765, ICTA 1988 to certain transactions in shares or debentures (see Inland Revenue Corporation Tax Manual CT 3449) and notification as required by s. 765A, ICTA 1988 of transactions falling within the European Capital Movements Directive (see Statement of Practice 2/92).

Please send application for consent or notification to:

Mark Ritchie
Revenue Policy, International
Business Tax Group (Treasury Consent)
Victory House
30–34 Kingsway
London WC2B 6ES

Advance Pricing Agreements

Under s. 85–87, FA 1999:

Application for an Advance Pricing Agreement relating to transfer pricing issues in accordance with s. 85–87, FA 1999 (See Statement of Practice 3/99).

Send application for agreement to:

Ian Wood
Revenue Policy, International
Business Tax Group (APAs)
Victory House
30–34 Kingsway
London WC2B 6ES

(For APAs involving oil taxation the contact continues to be, as stated in Statement of Practice SP3/99);

Janice Cross
Revenue Policy, International
Oil Taxation Office (APAs)
Melbourne House
Aldwych
London WC2B 4LL

Controlled Foreign Companies

Under s. 747–756 and Sch. 24–26, ICTA 1988:

Clearances in relation to Controlled Foreign Companies (see Corporation Tax Self Assessment: Controlled Foreign Companies Guidance Notes.

Send application for clearance to:

Stephen Hewitt
Revenue Policy, International
Business Tax Group (CFC Clearances)
Victory House
30–34 Kingsway
London WC2B 6ES

Funding Issues

Pre-transaction advice on funding issues under Tax Bulletins 17 and 37:

Send application for advice to:

Dave Smith
Revenue Policy, International
Business Tax Group (Advice on funding)
Victory House
30–34 Kingsway
London WC2B 6ES

Transactions in land

Under s. 35, ICTA 1988:

Confirmation of the taxpayer's view of the tax consequences of assigning a lease granted at under value.

Under s. 776, ICTA 1988:

Confirmation that s. 776, ICTA 1988 does not apply to gains made from transactions in land.

Please send applications for clearance to the Inspector of Taxes who deals with your returns.

Transfers of long term business between life assurance companies

Under s. 444A, ICTA 1988 and s. 211, TCGA 1992.

Where both parties are UK-resident life assurance companies, please send applications for clearance to:

Robert Peel
Revenue Policy, Business Tax
Room S16 West Wing
Somerset House
London WC2R 1LB

Where at least one party is a non-UK-resident company or is a friendly society, please send applications for clearance to:

Richard Thomas
Revenue Policy, Business Tax
Room S15 West Wing
Somerset House
London WC2R 1LB

Corporate Venturing Schemes

Under Sch. 15, FA 2000

Confirmation that the rules of the scheme (other than those applying to the investing company) will be satisfied.

Revenue Policy, Business Tax
Corporate Venturing Scheme Unit
Central Correspondence Unit
Room M26 New Wing
Somerset House
London WC2R 1LB

'One Stop Shop' for clearances

Following the recommendations made in the Review of Links with Business, since 1 April 2002 we have operated a 'One Stop Shop' approach to some clearances. More information on the Review can be found here (PDF).

The review recommendations are being implemented in stages but for demergers, purchase of own shares and S707 we can now deal with these clearances from a single application. What this means is that where clearance is sought under any one or more of s. 215, 225 & 707, ICTA 1988 you may send a single letter to the London addresses given below. **No extra copy is required** as we intend that the same person will deal with each of the clearances asked for.

It will help us if your letter makes clear at the outset what clearance is required. At present we are unable to deal with capital gains tax and other clearances from a single application so applications for clearance under the capital gains provisions should continue to be sent to Solihull at the address shown below. We are working to integrate the capital gains tax clearances and hope to say more on this within the coming months.

Non Market Sensitive

Mohini Sawhney
Fifth Floor
22 Kingsway
London WC2B 6NR

Market Sensitive

Ray McCann
Fifth Floor
22 Kingsway
London WC2B 6NR

Statutory approvals

Employee share schemes

Under Sch. 9, ICTA 1988.

Profit Sharing Schemes, Savings-Related Share Option Schemes & Company Share Option Plans.

Please send applications for approval to:

Kevin Meehan
Revenue Policy, Capital and Savings
Employee Share Schemes
2nd Floor, New Wing Somerset House
London WC2R 1LB

[See also our Share Schemes pages]

Pensions

Sections 590 & 591, ICTA 1988.

Occupational pensions, personal pensions, public sector schemes, FSAVC schemes & ex-gratia relevant payments.

Please send applications for approval to:

Inland Revenue
Pension Schemes Office
Yorke House
P.O. Box 62
Castle Meadow Road
Nottingham NG2 1BG

[See also our Pensions Schemes Office pages]

Qualifying Life Assurance Policies

Schedule 15, ICTA 1988.

Certification of qualifying life assurance policies

Please send applications for approval to:

Dolores Boase
Revenue Policy, Business Tax (Insurance)
Room S11, West Wing
Somerset House
London WC2B 6NR

Inland Revenue forms

For a complete list see http://www.inlandrevenue.gov.uk/menus/formmenu.htm.

Inland Revenue pamphlets

A full list of booklets and leaflets is available at http://www.inlandrevenue.gov.uk/leaflets/index.htm.

Retail Prices Index: general

The Retail Prices Index (RPI), issued by the Department of Employment, is used to calculate the indexation allowance for the purposes of calculating capital gains on corporation tax. (Since April 1998, the indexation allowance has ceased to be available when calculating gains liable to capital gains tax.) Certain personal and other reliefs are also linked to the RPI, subject to Parliament determining otherwise.

With effect from February 1987 the reference date to which the price level in each subsequent month is related was changed from 'January 1974 = 100' to 'January 1987 = 100'.

Movements in the RPI in the months after January 1987 are calculated with reference to January 1987 = 100. (With a base of January 1974 = 100, January 1987's RPI was 394.5). A new formula has been provided by the Department of Employment for calculating movements in the index over periods which span January 1987:

> 'The index for the later month (January 1987 = 100) is multiplied by the index for January 1987 (January 1974 = 100) and divided by the index for the earlier month (January 1974 = 100). 100 is subtracted to give the percentage change between the two months.'

CCH has prepared the following table in accordance with this formula:

	1982	1983	1984	1985	1986	1987	1988	1989	1990	1991
Jan.		82.61	86.84	91.20	96.25	100.0	103.3	111.0	119.5	130.2
Feb.		82.97	87.20	91.94	96.60	100.4	103.7	111.8	120.2	130.9
March	79.44	83.12	87.48	92.80	96.73	100.6	104.1	112.3	121.4	131.4
April	81.04	84.28	88.64	94.78	97.67	101.8	105.8	114.3	125.1	133.1
May	81.62	84.64	88.97	95.21	97.85	101.9	106.2	115.0	126.2	133.5
June	81.85	84.84	89.20	95.41	97.79	101.9	106.6	115.4	126.7	134.1
July	81.88	85.30	89.10	95.23	97.52	101.8	106.7	115.5	126.8	133.8
Aug.	81.90	85.68	89.94	95.49	97.82	102.1	107.9	115.8	128.1	134.1
Sept.	81.85	86.06	90.11	95.44	98.30	102.4	108.4	116.6	129.3	134.6
Oct.	82.26	86.36	90.67	95.59	98.45	102.9	109.5	117.5	130.3	135.1
Nov.	82.66	86.67	90.95	95.92	99.29	103.4	110.0	118.5	130.0	135.6
Dec.	82.51	86.89	90.87	96.05	99.62	103.3	110.3	118.8	129.9	135.7

	1992	1993	1994	1995	1996	1997	1998	1999	2000	2001
Jan.	135.6	137.9	141.3	146.0	150.2	154.4	159.5	163.4	166.6	171.1
Feb.	136.3	138.8	142.1	146.9	150.9	155.0	160.3	163.7	167.5	172.0
March	136.7	139.3	142.5	147.5	151.5	155.4	160.8	164.1	168.4	172.2
April	138.8	140.6	144.2	149.0	152.6	156.3	162.6	165.2	170.1	173.1
May	139.3	141.1	144.7	149.6	152.9	156.9	163.5	165.6	170.7	174.2
June	139.3	141.0	144.7	149.8	153.0	157.5	163.4	165.6	171.1	174.4
July	138.8	140.7	144.0	149.1	152.4	157.5	163.0	165.1	170.5	173.3
Aug.	138.9	141.3	144.7	149.9	153.1	158.5	163.7	165.5	170.5	174.0
Sept.	139.4	141.9	145.0	150.6	153.8	159.3	164.4	166.2	171.7	174.6
Oct.	139.9	141.8	145.2	149.8	153.8	159.5	164.5	166.5	171.6	174.3
Nov.	139.7	141.6	145.3	149.8	153.9	159.6	164.4	166.7	172.1	173.6
Dec.	139.2	141.9	146.0	150.7	154.4	160.0	164.4	167.3	172.2	173.4

	2002	2003	2004	2005	2006	2007	2008	2009	2010	2011
Jan.	173.3	178.4	183.1	188.9						
Feb.	173.8	179.3	183.8	189.6						
March	174.5	179.9	184.6	190.5						
April	175.7	181.2	185.7							
May	176.2	181.5	186.5							
June	176.2	181.3	186.8							
July	175.9	181.3	186.8							
Aug.	176.4	181.6	187.4							
Sept.	177.6	182.5	188.1							
Oct.	177.9	182.6	188.6							
Nov.	178.2	182.7	189.0							
Dec.	178.5	183.5	189.9							

The RPI figures for the month of December 1974 to December 1981 are given below for the purpose of calculating partnership retirement annuities .

	1974	1975	1976	1977	1978	1979	1980	1981
December	116.9	146.0	168.0	188.4	204.2	239.4	275.6	308.8

Indexation allowance up to 5 April 1998 (TCGA 1992, s. 53 and 54)

Indexation allowance in respect of changes shown by the retail prices indices for months after April 1998 shall be allowed only for the purposes of corporation tax. For disposals made by individuals, trustees and personal representatives after April 1998, indexation allowance up to 5 April 1998 and taper relief (see above) may be obtained.

The table below sets out the figure that is determined by the formula of (RD − RI)/RI where RD is the Retail Prices Index for April 1998 and RI is the Retail Prices Index for the later of March 1982 and the date that the item of relevant allowable expenditure was incurred. The indexation allowance is the aggregate of the indexed rise in each item of relevant allowable expenditure. In relation to each item of expenditure, the indexed rise is a sum produced by multiplying the amount of that item of expenditure by the appropriate figure in the table below.

	Jan.	Feb.	Mar.	Apr.	May	Jun.	Jul.	Aug.	Sep.	Oct.	Nov.	Dec.
1982	–	–	1.047	1.006	0.992	0.987	0.986	0.985	0.987	0.977	0.967	0.971
1983	0.968	0.960	0.956	0.929	0.921	0.917	0.906	0.898	0.889	0.883	0.876	0.871
1984	0.872	0.865	0.859	0.834	0.828	0.823	0.825	0.808	0.804	0.793	0.788	0.789
1985	0.783	0.769	0.752	0.716	0.708	0.704	0.707	0.703	0.704	0.701	0.695	0.693
1986	0.689	0.683	0.681	0.665	0.662	0.663	0.667	0.662	0.654	0.652	0.638	0.632
1987	0.626	0.620	0.616	0.597	0.596	0.596	0.597	0.593	0.588	0.580	0.573	0.574
1988	0.574	0.568	0.562	0.537	0.531	0.525	0.524	0.507	0.500	0.485	0.478	0.474
1989	0.465	0.454	0.448	0.423	0.414	0.409	0.408	0.404	0.395	0.384	0.372	0.369
1990	0.361	0.353	0.339	0.300	0.288	0.283	0.282	0.269	0.258	0.248	0.251	0.252
1991	0.249	0.242	0.237	0.222	0.218	0.213	0.215	0.213	0.208	0.204	0.199	0.198
1992	0.199	0.193	0.189	0.171	0.167	0.167	0.171	0.171	0.166	0.162	0.164	0.168
1993	0.179	0.171	0.167	0.156	0.152	0.153	0.156	0.151	0.146	0.147	0.148	0.146
1994	0.151	0.144	0.141	0.128	0.124	0.124	0.129	0.124	0.121	0.120	0.119	0.114
1995	0.114	0.107	0.102	0.091	0.087	0.085	0.091	0.085	0.080	0.085	0.085	0.079
1996	0.083	0.078	0.073	0.066	0.063	0.063	0.067	0.062	0.057	0.057	0.057	0.053
1997	0.053	0.049	0.046	0.040	0.036	0.032	0.032	0.026	0.021	0.019	0.019	0.016
1998	0.019	0.014	0.011	–	–	–	–	–	–	–	–	–

Disposals since April 2004

Tables follow showing the indexed rise to be used for disposals between April 2004 and March 2005. The amount of indexation allowance is restricted where the indexation allowance gives rise to a loss.

RPI: 04/04 to 03/05

RD Month (April 2004–March 2005) January 1987 = 100

RI Month	2004 April	May	June	July	Aug.	Sept.	Oct.	Nov.	Dec.	2005 Jan.	Feb.	Mar.
1982 *March*	1.338	1.348	1.351	1.351	1.359	1.368	1.374	1.379	1.390	1.378	1.387	1.398
April	1.291	1.301	1.305	1.305	1.312	1.321	1.327	1.332	1.343	1.331	1.340	1.351
May	1.275	1.285	1.289	1.289	1.296	1.305	1.311	1.316	1.327	1.314	1.323	1.334
June	1.269	1.279	1.282	1.282	1.290	1.298	1.304	1.309	1.320	1.308	1.316	1.327
July	1.268	1.278	1.281	1.281	1.289	1.297	1.303	1.308	1.319	1.306	1.316	1.327
Aug.	1.267	1.277	1.280	1.280	1.288	1.298	1.303	1.308	1.319	1.306	1.315	1.326
Sept.	1.269	1.279	1.282	1.282	1.290	1.299	1.304	1.309	1.320	1.308	1.316	1.327
Oct.	1.258	1.267	1.271	1.271	1.278	1.287	1.293	1.298	1.309	1.296	1.305	1.316
Nov.	1.247	1.256	1.260	1.260	1.267	1.276	1.282	1.286	1.297	1.285	1.294	1.305
Dec.	1.251	1.260	1.264	1.264	1.271	1.280	1.286	1.291	1.302	1.289	1.298	1.309
1983 *Jan.*	1.248	1.258	1.261	1.261	1.268	1.277	1.283	1.288	1.299	1.287	1.295	1.306
Feb.	1.238	1.248	1.252	1.252	1.259	1.267	1.273	1.278	1.289	1.277	1.285	1.296
March	1.234	1.244	1.247	1.247	1.255	1.263	1.269	1.274	1.285	1.273	1.281	1.292
April	1.203	1.213	1.216	1.216	1.223	1.232	1.238	1.242	1.253	1.241	1.250	1.260
May	1.194	1.203	1.207	1.207	1.214	1.222	1.228	1.233	1.244	1.232	1.240	1.251
June	1.189	1.198	1.202	1.202	1.209	1.217	1.223	1.228	1.238	1.227	1.235	1.245
July	1.177	1.186	1.190	1.190	1.197	1.205	1.211	1.216	1.226	1.215	1.223	1.233
Aug.	1.167	1.177	1.180	1.180	1.187	1.195	1.201	1.206	1.216	1.205	1.213	1.223
Sept.	1.158	1.167	1.171	1.171	1.178	1.186	1.192	1.196	1.207	1.195	1.203	1.214
Oct.	1.150	1.160	1.163	1.163	1.170	1.178	1.184	1.188	1.199	1.187	1.195	1.206
Nov.	1.143	1.152	1.155	1.155	1.162	1.170	1.176	1.181	1.191	1.180	1.188	1.198
Dec.	1.137	1.146	1.150	1.150	1.157	1.165	1.170	1.175	1.185	1.174	1.182	1.192
1984 *Jan.*	1.138	1.148	1.151	1.151	1.158	1.166	1.172	1.176	1.187	1.175	1.183	1.194
Feb.	1.130	1.139	1.142	1.142	1.149	1.157	1.163	1.167	1.178	1.166	1.174	1.185
March	1.123	1.132	1.135	1.135	1.142	1.150	1.156	1.161	1.171	1.159	1.167	1.178
April	1.095	1.104	1.107	1.107	1.114	1.122	1.128	1.132	1.142	1.131	1.139	1.149
May	1.087	1.096	1.100	1.100	1.106	1.114	1.120	1.124	1.134	1.123	1.131	1.141
June	1.082	1.091	1.094	1.094	1.101	1.109	1.114	1.119	1.129	1.118	1.126	1.136
July	1.084	1.093	1.097	1.097	1.103	1.111	1.117	1.121	1.131	1.120	1.128	1.138
Aug.	1.065	1.074	1.077	1.077	1.084	1.091	1.097	1.101	1.111	1.100	1.108	1.118
Sept.	1.061	1.070	1.073	1.073	1.080	1.087	1.093	1.097	1.107	1.096	1.104	1.114
Oct.	1.048	1.057	1.060	1.060	1.067	1.075	1.080	1.084	1.094	1.083	1.091	1.101
Nov.	1.042	1.051	1.054	1.054	1.060	1.068	1.074	1.078	1.088	1.077	1.085	1.095
Dec.	1.043	1.052	1.056	1.056	1.062	1.070	1.075	1.080	1.090	1.079	1.086	1.096

RD Month (April 2004–March 2005) January 1987 = 100

RI Month	2004 April	May	June	July	Aug.	Sept.	Oct.	Nov.	Dec.	2005 Jan.	Feb.	Mar.
1985 Jan.	1.036	1.045	1.048	1.048	1.055	1.062	1.068	1.072	1.082	1.071	1.079	1.089
Feb.	1.020	1.029	1.032	1.032	1.038	1.046	1.051	1.056	1.065	1.055	1.062	1.072
March	1.001	1.010	1.013	1.013	1.019	1.027	1.032	1.037	1.046	1.035	1.043	1.053
April	0.959	0.968	0.971	0.971	0.977	0.985	0.990	0.994	1.004	0.993	1.000	1.010
May	0.950	0.959	0.962	0.962	0.968	0.976	0.981	0.985	0.995	0.984	0.991	1.001
June	0.945	0.955	0.958	0.958	0.964	0.971	0.977	0.981	0.990	0.980	0.987	0.997
July	0.950	0.958	0.961	0.961	0.968	0.975	0.980	0.985	0.994	0.984	0.991	1.000
Aug.	0.945	0.953	0.956	0.956	0.963	0.970	0.975	0.979	0.989	0.973	0.986	0.995
Sept.	0.946	0.954	0.957	0.957	0.964	0.971	0.976	0.980	0.990	0.979	0.987	0.996
Oct.	0.943	0.951	0.954	0.954	0.960	0.968	0.973	0.977	0.987	0.976	0.983	0.993
Nov.	0.936	0.944	0.947	0.947	0.954	0.961	0.966	0.970	0.980	0.969	0.977	0.986
Dec.	0.933	0.942	0.945	0.945	0.951	0.958	0.964	0.968	0.977	0.967	0.974	0.983
1986 Jan.	0.929	0.938	0.941	0.941	0.947	0.954	0.960	0.964	0.973	0.963	0.970	0.979
Feb.	0.922	0.931	0.934	0.934	0.940	0.947	0.952	0.956	0.966	0.955	0.963	0.972
March	0.920	0.928	0.931	0.931	0.937	0.945	0.950	0.954	0.963	0.953	0.960	0.969
April	0.901	0.910	0.913	0.913	0.919	0.926	0.931	0.935	0.944	0.934	0.941	0.950
May	0.898	0.906	0.909	0.909	0.915	0.922	0.928	0.932	0.941	0.931	0.938	0.947
June	0.899	0.907	0.910	0.910	0.916	0.923	0.929	0.933	0.942	0.932	0.939	0.948
July	0.904	0.913	0.916	0.916	0.922	0.929	0.934	0.938	0.947	0.937	0.944	0.954
Aug.	0.898	0.907	0.910	0.910	0.916	0.923	0.928	0.932	0.941	0.931	0.938	0.947
Sept.	0.889	0.897	0.900	0.900	0.906	0.913	0.919	0.923	0.932	0.922	0.929	0.938
Oct.	0.886	0.894	0.897	0.897	0.903	0.911	0.916	0.920	0.929	0.919	0.926	0.935
Nov.	0.870	0.878	0.881	0.881	0.887	0.894	0.899	0.904	0.913	0.903	0.910	0.919
Dec.	0.864	0.872	0.875	0.875	0.881	0.888	0.893	0.897	0.906	0.896	0.903	0.912
1987 Jan.	0.857	0.865	0.868	0.868	0.874	0.881	0.886	0.890	0.899	0.889	0.896	0.905
Feb.	0.850	0.858	0.861	0.861	0.867	0.874	0.878	0.882	0.891	0.881	0.888	0.897
March	0.846	0.854	0.857	0.857	0.863	0.870	0.875	0.879	0.888	0.873	0.885	0.894
April	0.824	0.832	0.835	0.835	0.841	0.848	0.853	0.857	0.865	0.856	0.862	0.871
May	0.822	0.830	0.833	0.833	0.839	0.846	0.851	0.855	0.864	0.854	0.861	0.869
June	0.824	0.832	0.835	0.835	0.841	0.848	0.853	0.857	0.865	0.856	0.862	0.871
July	0.819	0.827	0.830	0.830	0.835	0.842	0.847	0.851	0.860	0.850	0.857	0.866
Aug.	0.813	0.821	0.824	0.824	0.830	0.837	0.842	0.846	0.854	0.845	0.852	0.860
Sept.	0.805	0.812	0.815	0.815	0.821	0.828	0.833	0.837	0.845	0.836	0.843	0.851
Oct.	0.796	0.804	0.807	0.807	0.812	0.819	0.824	0.828	0.837	0.827	0.834	0.842
Nov.	0.798	0.805	0.808	0.808	0.814	0.821	0.826	0.830	0.838	0.829	0.835	0.844

RD Month (April 2004–March 2005) January 1987 = 100

RI Month	2004 April	May	June	July	Aug.	Sept.	Oct.	Nov.	Dec.	2005 Jan.	Feb.	Mar.
1988 Jan.	0.798	0.805	0.808	0.808	0.814	0.821	0.826	0.830	0.838	0.829	0.835	0.844
Feb.	0.791	0.798	0.801	0.801	0.800	0.814	0.819	0.823	0.831	0.822	0.828	0.837
March	0.784	0.792	0.794	0.794	0.800	0.807	0.812	0.816	0.824	0.815	0.821	0.830
April	0.755	0.763	0.766	0.766	0.771	0.778	0.783	0.786	0.795	0.785	0.792	0.801
May	0.749	0.756	0.759	0.759	0.765	0.771	0.776	0.780	0.788	0.779	0.785	0.794
June	0.742	0.750	0.752	0.752	0.758	0.765	0.769	0.773	0.781	0.772	0.779	0.787
July	0.740	0.748	0.751	0.751	0.756	0.763	0.768	0.771	0.780	0.770	0.777	0.785
Aug.	0.721	0.728	0.731	0.731	0.737	0.743	0.748	0.752	0.760	0.751	0.757	0.766
Sept.	0.713	0.720	0.723	0.723	0.729	0.735	0.740	0.744	0.752	0.743	0.749	0.757
Oct.	0.696	0.703	0.706	0.706	0.711	0.718	0.722	0.726	0.734	0.725	0.732	0.740
Nov.	0.688	0.695	0.698	0.698	0.704	0.710	0.715	0.718	0.726	0.717	0.724	0.732
Dec.	0.684	0.691	0.694	0.694	0.699	0.705	0.710	0.714	0.722	0.713	0.719	0.727
1989 Jan.	0.673	0.680	0.683	0.683	0.688	0.695	0.699	0.703	0.711	0.702	0.708	0.716
Feb.	0.661	0.668	0.671	0.671	0.676	0.682	0.687	0.691	0.699	0.690	0.696	0.704
March	0.654	0.661	0.663	0.663	0.669	0.675	0.679	0.683	0.691	0.682	0.688	0.696
April	0.625	0.632	0.634	0.634	0.640	0.646	0.650	0.654	0.661	0.653	0.659	0.667
May	0.615	0.622	0.624	0.624	0.630	0.636	0.640	0.643	0.651	0.643	0.649	0.657
June	0.609	0.616	0.619	0.619	0.624	0.630	0.634	0.638	0.646	0.637	0.643	0.651
July	0.608	0.615	0.617	0.617	0.623	0.629	0.633	0.636	0.644	0.635	0.642	0.649
Aug.	0.604	0.611	0.613	0.613	0.618	0.624	0.629	0.632	0.640	0.631	0.637	0.645
Sept.	0.593	0.599	0.602	0.602	0.607	0.613	0.617	0.621	0.629	0.620	0.626	0.634
Oct.	0.580	0.587	0.590	0.590	0.595	0.601	0.605	0.609	0.616	0.608	0.614	0.621
Nov.	0.567	0.574	0.576	0.576	0.581	0.587	0.592	0.595	0.603	0.594	0.600	0.608
Dec.	0.563	0.570	0.572	0.572	0.577	0.583	0.588	0.591	0.598	0.590	0.596	0.604
1990 Jan.	0.554	0.561	0.563	0.563	0.568	0.574	0.578	0.582	0.589	0.581	0.587	0.594
Feb.	0.545	0.552	0.554	0.554	0.559	0.565	0.569	0.572	0.580	0.572	0.577	0.585
March	0.530	0.536	0.539	0.539	0.544	0.549	0.554	0.557	0.564	0.556	0.562	0.569
April	0.484	0.491	0.493	0.493	0.498	0.504	0.508	0.511	0.518	0.510	0.516	0.523
May	0.471	0.478	0.480	0.480	0.485	0.490	0.494	0.498	0.505	0.497	0.502	0.510
June	0.466	0.472	0.474	0.474	0.479	0.485	0.489	0.492	0.499	0.491	0.496	0.504
July	0.465	0.471	0.473	0.473	0.478	0.483	0.487	0.491	0.498	0.490	0.495	0.502
Aug.	0.450	0.456	0.458	0.458	0.463	0.468	0.472	0.475	0.482	0.475	0.480	0.487
Sept.	0.436	0.442	0.445	0.445	0.449	0.455	0.459	0.462	0.469	0.461	0.466	0.473
Oct.	0.425	0.431	0.434	0.434	0.438	0.444	0.447	0.450	0.457	0.450	0.455	0.462
Nov.	0.428	0.435	0.437	0.437	0.442	0.447	0.451	0.454	0.461	0.453	0.458	0.465
Dec.	0.430	0.436	0.438	0.438	0.443	0.448	0.452	0.455	0.462	0.454	0.460	0.467

RD Month (April 2004–March 2005) January 1987 = 100

RI Month	2004 April	May	June	July	Aug.	Sept.	Oct.	Nov.	Dec.	2005 Jan.	Feb.	Mar.
1991 Jan.	0.426	0.432	0.435	0.435	0.439	0.445	0.449	0.452	0.459	0.451	0.456	0.463
Feb.	0.419	0.425	0.427	0.427	0.432	0.437	0.441	0.444	0.451	0.443	0.448	0.455
March	0.413	0.419	0.422	0.422	0.426	0.432	0.435	0.438	0.445	0.438	0.443	0.450
April	0.395	0.401	0.403	0.403	0.408	0.413	0.417	0.420	0.427	0.419	0.424	0.431
May	0.391	0.397	0.399	0.399	0.404	0.409	0.413	0.416	0.422	0.415	0.420	0.427
June	0.385	0.391	0.393	0.393	0.397	0.403	0.406	0.409	0.416	0.409	0.414	0.421
July	0.388	0.394	0.396	0.396	0.401	0.406	0.410	0.413	0.419	0.412	0.417	0.424
Aug.	0.385	0.391	0.393	0.393	0.397	0.403	0.406	0.409	0.416	0.409	0.414	0.421
Sept.	0.380	0.386	0.388	0.388	0.392	0.397	0.401	0.404	0.411	0.403	0.409	0.415
Oct.	0.375	0.380	0.383	0.383	0.387	0.392	0.396	0.399	0.406	0.398	0.403	0.410
Nov.	0.369	0.375	0.377	0.378	0.382	0.387	0.391	0.394	0.400	0.393	0.398	0.405
Dec.	0.368	0.374	0.377	0.378	0.381	0.386	0.390	0.393	0.399	0.392	0.397	0.404
1992 Jan.	0.369	0.375	0.378	0.378	0.382	0.387	0.391	0.394	0.400	0.393	0.398	0.405
Feb.	0.362	0.368	0.371	0.371	0.375	0.380	0.384	0.387	0.393	0.386	0.391	0.398
March	0.358	0.364	0.366	0.366	0.371	0.376	0.380	0.383	0.389	0.382	0.387	0.394
April	0.338	0.344	0.346	0.346	0.350	0.355	0.359	0.362	0.368	0.361	0.366	0.372
May	0.333	0.339	0.341	0.341	0.345	0.350	0.354	0.357	0.363	0.356	0.361	0.368
June	0.333	0.339	0.341	0.341	0.345	0.350	0.354	0.357	0.363	0.356	0.361	0.368
July	0.338	0.344	0.346	0.346	0.350	0.355	0.359	0.362	0.368	0.361	0.366	0.372
Aug.	0.337	0.343	0.345	0.345	0.349	0.354	0.358	0.361	0.367	0.360	0.365	0.371
Sept.	0.332	0.338	0.340	0.340	0.344	0.349	0.353	0.356	0.362	0.355	0.360	0.367
Oct.	0.327	0.333	0.335	0.335	0.340	0.345	0.348	0.351	0.357	0.350	0.355	0.362
Nov.	0.329	0.335	0.337	0.337	0.341	0.346	0.350	0.353	0.359	0.352	0.357	0.364
Dec.	0.334	0.340	0.342	0.342	0.346	0.351	0.355	0.358	0.364	0.357	0.362	0.369
1993 Jan.	0.347	0.352	0.355	0.355	0.359	0.364	0.368	0.371	0.377	0.370	0.375	0.381
Feb.	0.338	0.344	0.346	0.346	0.350	0.355	0.359	0.362	0.368	0.361	0.366	0.372
March	0.333	0.339	0.341	0.341	0.345	0.350	0.354	0.357	0.363	0.356	0.361	0.368
April	0.321	0.326	0.329	0.329	0.333	0.338	0.341	0.344	0.351	0.344	0.349	0.355
May	0.316	0.322	0.324	0.324	0.328	0.333	0.337	0.339	0.346	0.339	0.344	0.350
June	0.317	0.323	0.325	0.325	0.329	0.334	0.338	0.340	0.347	0.340	0.345	0.351
July	0.320	0.326	0.328	0.328	0.332	0.337	0.340	0.343	0.350	0.343	0.348	0.354
Aug.	0.314	0.320	0.322	0.322	0.326	0.331	0.335	0.338	0.344	0.337	0.342	0.348
Sept.	0.309	0.314	0.316	0.316	0.321	0.326	0.329	0.332	0.338	0.331	0.336	0.342
Oct.	0.310	0.315	0.317	0.317	0.322	0.327	0.330	0.333	0.339	0.332	0.337	0.343
Nov.	0.311	0.317	0.319	0.319	0.323	0.328	0.332	0.335	0.341	0.334	0.339	0.345
Dec.	0.309	0.314	0.316	0.316	0.321	0.326	0.329	0.332	0.338	0.331	0.336	0.342

RD Month (April 2004–March 2005) January 1987 = 100

RI Month	2004 April	May	June	July	Aug.	Sept.	Oct.	Nov.	Dec.	2005 Jan.	Feb.	Mar.
1994 Jan.	0.314	0.320	0.322	0.322	0.326	0.331	0.335	0.338	0.344	0.337	0.342	0.348
Feb.	0.307	0.312	0.315	0.315	0.319	0.324	0.327	0.330	0.336	0.329	0.334	0.341
March	0.303	0.309	0.311	0.311	0.315	0.320	0.324	0.326	0.333	0.326	0.331	0.337
April	0.288	0.293	0.295	0.295	0.300	0.304	0.308	0.311	0.317	0.310	0.315	0.321
May	0.283	0.289	0.291	0.291	0.295	0.300	0.303	0.306	0.312	0.305	0.310	0.317
June	0.283	0.289	0.291	0.291	0.295	0.300	0.303	0.306	0.312	0.305	0.310	0.317
July	0.290	0.295	0.297	0.297	0.301	0.306	0.310	0.313	0.319	0.312	0.317	0.323
Aug.	0.283	0.289	0.291	0.291	0.295	0.300	0.303	0.306	0.312	0.305	0.310	0.317
Sept.	0.281	0.286	0.288	0.288	0.292	0.297	0.301	0.303	0.310	0.303	0.308	0.314
Oct.	0.279	0.284	0.287	0.287	0.291	0.295	0.299	0.302	0.308	0.301	0.306	0.312
Nov.	0.278	0.284	0.286	0.286	0.290	0.295	0.298	0.301	0.307	0.300	0.305	0.311
Dec.	0.272	0.277	0.279	0.279	0.284	0.288	0.292	0.295	0.301	0.294	0.299	0.305
1995 Jan.	0.272	0.277	0.279	0.279	0.284	0.288	0.292	0.295	0.301	0.294	0.299	0.305
Feb.	0.264	0.270	0.272	0.272	0.276	0.280	0.284	0.287	0.293	0.286	0.291	0.297
March	0.259	0.264	0.266	0.266	0.271	0.275	0.279	0.281	0.287	0.281	0.285	0.292
April	0.246	0.252	0.254	0.254	0.258	0.262	0.266	0.268	0.274	0.268	0.272	0.279
May	0.241	0.247	0.249	0.249	0.253	0.257	0.261	0.263	0.269	0.263	0.267	0.273
June	0.240	0.245	0.247	0.247	0.251	0.256	0.259	0.262	0.268	0.261	0.266	0.272
July	0.245	0.251	0.253	0.253	0.257	0.262	0.265	0.268	0.274	0.267	0.272	0.278
Aug.	0.239	0.244	0.246	0.246	0.250	0.255	0.258	0.261	0.267	0.260	0.265	0.271
Sept.	0.233	0.238	0.240	0.240	0.244	0.249	0.252	0.255	0.261	0.254	0.259	0.265
Oct.	0.240	0.245	0.247	0.247	0.251	0.256	0.259	0.262	0.268	0.261	0.266	0.272
Nov.	0.240	0.245	0.247	0.247	0.251	0.256	0.259	0.262	0.268	0.261	0.266	0.272
Dec.	0.232	0.238	0.240	0.240	0.244	0.248	0.251	0.254	0.260	0.253	0.258	0.264
1996 Jan.	0.236	0.242	0.244	0.244	0.248	0.252	0.256	0.258	0.264	0.258	0.262	0.268
Feb.	0.231	0.236	0.238	0.238	0.242	0.247	0.250	0.252	0.258	0.252	0.256	0.262
March	0.226	0.231	0.233	0.233	0.237	0.242	0.245	0.248	0.253	0.247	0.251	0.257
April	0.217	0.222	0.224	0.224	0.228	0.233	0.236	0.239	0.244	0.238	0.242	0.248
May	0.215	0.220	0.222	0.222	0.226	0.230	0.233	0.236	0.242	0.235	0.240	0.246
June	0.214	0.219	0.221	0.221	0.225	0.229	0.233	0.235	0.241	0.235	0.239	0.245
July	0.219	0.224	0.226	0.226	0.230	0.234	0.238	0.240	0.246	0.240	0.244	0.250
Aug.	0.213	0.218	0.220	0.220	0.224	0.229	0.232	0.234	0.240	0.234	0.238	0.244
Sept.	0.207	0.213	0.215	0.215	0.218	0.223	0.226	0.229	0.235	0.228	0.233	0.239
Oct.	0.207	0.213	0.215	0.215	0.218	0.223	0.226	0.229	0.235	0.228	0.233	0.239
Nov.	0.207	0.212	0.214	0.214	0.218	0.222	0.225	0.228	0.234	0.227	0.232	0.238
Dec.	0.203	0.208	0.210	0.210	0.214	0.218	0.222	0.224	0.230	0.223	0.228	0.234

RD Month (April 2004–March 2005) January 1987 = 100

RI Month	2004 April	May	June	July	Aug.	Sept.	Oct.	Nov.	Dec.	2005 Jan.	Feb.	Mar.
1997 Jan.	0.203	0.208	0.210	0.210	0.214	0.218	0.222	0.224	0.230	0.223	0.228	0.234
Feb.	0.198	0.203	0.205	0.205	0.209	0.214	0.217	0.219	0.225	0.219	0.223	0.229
1997 March	0.195	0.200	0.202	0.202	0.206	0.210	0.214	0.216	0.222	0.216	0.220	0.226
April	0.188	0.193	0.195	0.195	0.199	0.203	0.207	0.209	0.215	0.209	0.213	0.219
May	0.184	0.189	0.191	0.191	0.194	0.199	0.202	0.205	0.210	0.204	0.208	0.214
June	0.179	0.184	0.186	0.186	0.190	0.194	0.197	0.200	0.206	0.199	0.204	0.210
July	0.179	0.184	0.186	0.186	0.190	0.194	0.197	0.200	0.206	0.199	0.204	0.210
Aug.	0.172	0.177	0.179	0.179	0.182	0.187	0.190	0.192	0.198	0.192	0.196	0.202
Sept.	0.166	0.171	0.173	0.173	0.176	0.181	0.184	0.186	0.192	0.186	0.190	0.196
Oct.	0.164	0.169	0.171	0.171	0.175	0.179	0.182	0.185	0.191	0.184	0.189	0.194
Nov.	0.164	0.169	0.170	0.170	0.174	0.179	0.182	0.184	0.190	0.184	0.188	0.194
Dec.	0.161	0.166	0.168	0.168	0.171	0.176	0.179	0.181	0.187	0.181	0.185	0.191
1998 Jan.	0.164	0.169	0.171	0.171	0.175	0.179	0.182	0.185	0.191	0.184	0.189	0.194
Feb.	0.158	0.163	0.165	0.165	0.169	0.173	0.177	0.179	0.185	0.178	0.183	0.188
March	0.155	0.160	0.162	0.162	0.165	0.170	0.173	0.175	0.181	0.175	0.179	0.185
April	0.142	0.147	0.149	0.149	0.153	0.157	0.160	0.162	0.168	0.162	0.166	0.172
May	0.136	0.141	0.143	0.143	0.146	0.150	0.154	0.156	0.161	0.155	0.160	0.165
June	0.136	0.141	0.143	0.143	0.147	0.151	0.154	0.157	0.162	0.156	0.160	0.166
July	0.139	0.144	0.146	0.146	0.150	0.154	0.157	0.160	0.165	0.159	0.163	0.169
Aug.	0.134	0.139	0.141	0.141	0.145	0.149	0.152	0.155	0.160	0.154	0.158	0.164
Sept.	0.130	0.134	0.136	0.136	0.140	0.144	0.147	0.150	0.155	0.149	0.153	0.159
Oct.	0.129	0.134	0.136	0.136	0.139	0.143	0.147	0.149	0.154	0.148	0.153	0.158
Nov.	0.130	0.134	0.136	0.136	0.140	0.144	0.147	0.150	0.155	0.149	0.153	0.159
Dec.	0.130	0.134	0.136	0.136	0.140	0.144	0.147	0.150	0.155	0.149	0.153	0.159
1999 Jan.	0.136	0.141	0.143	0.143	0.147	0.151	0.154	0.157	0.162	0.156	0.160	0.166
Feb.	0.134	0.139	0.141	0.141	0.145	0.149	0.152	0.155	0.160	0.154	0.158	0.164
March	0.132	0.137	0.138	0.138	0.142	0.146	0.149	0.152	0.157	0.151	0.155	0.161
April	0.124	0.129	0.131	0.131	0.134	0.139	0.142	0.144	0.150	0.143	0.148	0.153
May	0.121	0.126	0.128	0.128	0.132	0.136	0.139	0.141	0.147	0.141	0.145	0.150
June	0.121	0.126	0.128	0.128	0.132	0.136	0.139	0.141	0.147	0.141	0.145	0.150
July	0.125	0.130	0.131	0.131	0.135	0.139	0.142	0.145	0.150	0.144	0.148	0.154
Aug.	0.122	0.127	0.129	0.129	0.132	0.137	0.140	0.142	0.147	0.141	0.146	0.151
Sept.	0.117	0.122	0.124	0.124	0.128	0.132	0.135	0.137	0.143	0.137	0.141	0.146
Oct.	0.115	0.120	0.122	0.122	0.126	0.130	0.133	0.135	0.141	0.135	0.139	0.144
Nov.	0.114	0.119	0.121	0.121	0.124	0.128	0.131	0.134	0.139	0.133	0.137	0.143
Dec.	0.110	0.115	0.117	0.117	0.120	0.124	0.127	0.130	0.135	0.129	0.133	0.139

RD Month (April 2004–March 2005) January 1987 = 100

RI Month	2004 April	May	June	July	Aug.	Sept.	Oct.	Nov.	Dec.	2005 Jan.	Feb.	Mar.
2000 Jan.	0.115	0.119	0.121	0.121	0.125	0.129	0.132	0.134	0.140	0.134	0.138	0.143
Feb.	0.109	0.113	0.115	0.115	0.119	0.123	0.126	0.128	0.134	0.128	0.132	0.137
March	0.103	0.107	0.109	0.109	0.113	0.117	0.120	0.122	0.128	0.122	0.126	0.131
April	0.092	0.096	0.098	0.098	0.102	0.106	0.109	0.111	0.116	0.111	0.115	0.120
May	0.088	0.093	0.094	0.094	0.098	0.102	0.105	0.107	0.112	0.107	0.111	0.116
June	0.085	0.090	0.092	0.092	0.095	0.099	0.102	0.105	0.110	0.104	0.108	0.113
July	0.089	0.094	0.096	0.096	0.099	0.103	0.106	0.109	0.114	0.108	0.112	0.117
Aug.	0.089	0.094	0.096	0.096	0.099	0.103	0.106	0.109	0.114	0.108	0.112	0.117
Sept.	0.082	0.086	0.088	0.088	0.091	0.096	0.098	0.101	0.106	0.100	0.104	0.109
Oct.	0.082	0.087	0.089	0.089	0.092	0.096	0.099	0.101	0.107	0.101	0.105	0.110
Nov.	0.079	0.084	0.085	0.085	0.089	0.093	0.096	0.098	0.103	0.098	0.102	0.107
Dec.	0.078	0.083	0.085	0.085	0.088	0.092	0.095	0.098	0.103	0.097	0.101	0.106
2001 Jan.	0.085	0.090	0.092	0.092	0.095	0.099	0.102	0.105	0.110	0.104	0.108	0.113
Feb.	0.080	0.084	0.086	0.086	0.090	0.094	0.097	0.099	0.104	0.098	0.102	0.108
March	0.078	0.083	0.085	0.085	0.088	0.092	0.095	0.098	0.103	0.097	0.101	0.106
April	0.073	0.077	0.079	0.079	0.083	0.087	0.090	0.092	0.097	0.091	0.095	0.101
May	0.066	0.071	0.072	0.072	0.076	0.080	0.083	0.085	0.090	0.084	0.088	0.094
June	0.065	0.069	0.071	0.071	0.075	0.079	0.081	0.084	0.089	0.083	0.087	0.092
July	0.072	0.076	0.078	0.078	0.081	0.085	0.088	0.091	0.096	0.090	0.094	0.099
Aug.	0.067	0.072	0.074	0.074	0.077	0.081	0.084	0.086	0.091	0.086	0.090	0.095
Sept.	0.064	0.068	0.070	0.070	0.073	0.077	0.080	0.082	0.088	0.082	0.086	0.091
Oct.	0.065	0.070	0.072	0.072	0.075	0.079	0.082	0.084	0.090	0.084	0.088	0.093
Nov.	0.070	0.074	0.076	0.076	0.079	0.084	0.086	0.089	0.094	0.088	0.092	0.097
Dec.	0.071	0.076	0.077	0.077	0.081	0.085	0.088	0.090	0.095	0.089	0.093	0.099
2002 Jan.	0.072	0.076	0.078	0.078	0.081	0.085	0.088	0.091	0.096	0.090	0.094	0.099
Feb.	0.068	0.073	0.075	0.075	0.078	0.082	0.085	0.087	0.093	0.087	0.091	0.096
March	0.064	0.069	0.070	0.070	0.074	0.078	0.081	0.083	0.088	0.083	0.087	0.092
April	0.057	0.061	0.063	0.063	0.067	0.071	0.073	0.076	0.081	0.075	0.079	0.084
May	0.054	0.058	0.060	0.060	0.064	0.068	0.070	0.073	0.078	0.072	0.076	0.081
June	0.054	0.058	0.060	0.060	0.064	0.068	0.070	0.073	0.078	0.072	0.076	0.081
July	0.056	0.060	0.062	0.062	0.065	0.069	0.072	0.074	0.080	0.074	0.078	0.083
Aug.	0.053	0.057	0.059	0.059	0.062	0.066	0.069	0.071	0.077	0.071	0.075	0.080
Sept.	0.046	0.050	0.052	0.052	0.055	0.059	0.062	0.064	0.069	0.064	0.068	0.073

RD Month (April 2004–March 2005) January 1987 = 100

RI Month	2004 April	May	June	July	Aug.	Sept.	Oct.	Nov.	Dec.	2005 Jan.	Feb.	Mar.
Oct.	0.044	0.048	0.050	0.050	0.053	0.057	0.060	0.062	0.067	0.062	0.066	0.071
Nov.	0.042	0.047	0.048	0.048	0.052	0.056	0.058	0.061	0.066	0.060	0.064	0.069
Dec.	0.040	0.045	0.046	0.046	0.050	0.054	0.057	0.059	0.064	0.058	0.062	0.067
2003 Jan.	0.041	0.045	0.047	0.047	0.050	0.054	0.057	0.059	0.064	0.059	0.063	0.068
Feb.	0.036	0.040	0.042	0.042	0.045	0.049	0.052	0.054	0.059	0.054	0.057	0.062
Mar.	0.032	0.037	0.038	0.038	0.042	0.046	0.048	0.051	0.056	0.050	0.054	0.059
April	0.025	0.029	0.031	0.031	0.034	0.038	0.041	0.043	0.048	0.042	0.046	0.051
May	0.023	0.028	0.029	0.029	0.033	0.036	0.039	0.041	0.046	0.041	0.045	0.050
June	0.024	0.029	0.030	0.030	0.034	0.038	0.040	0.042	0.047	0.042	0.046	0.051
July	0.024	0.029	0.030	0.030	0.034	0.038	0.040	0.042	0.047	0.042	0.046	0.051
Aug.	0.023	0.027	0.029	0.029	0.032	0.036	0.039	0.041	0.046	0.040	0.044	0.049
Sep.	0.018	0.022	0.024	0.024	0.027	0.031	0.033	0.036	0.041	0.035	0.039	0.044
Oct.	0.017	0.021	0.023	0.023	0.026	0.030	0.033	0.035	0.040	0.035	0.038	0.043
Nov.	0.016	0.021	0.022	0.022	0.026	0.030	0.032	0.034	0.039	0.034	0.038	0.043
Dec.	0.012	0.016	0.018	0.018	0.021	0.025	0.028	0.030	0.035	0.029	0.033	0.038
2004 Jan.	0.014	0.019	0.020	0.020	0.023	0.027	0.030	0.032	0.037	0.032	0.035	0.040
Feb.	0.010	0.015	0.016	0.016	0.020	0.023	0.026	0.028	0.033	0.028	0.032	0.036
Mar.	0.006	0.010	0.012	0.012	0.015	0.019	0.022	0.024	0.029	0.023	0.027	0.032
April	—	0.004	0.006	0.006	0.009	0.013	0.016	0.018	0.023	0.017	0.021	0.026
May	—	—	0.002	0.002	0.005	0.009	0.011	0.013	0.018	0.013	0.017	0.021
June	—	—	—	Nil	0.003	0.007	0.010	0.012	0.017	0.011	0.015	0.020
July	—	—	—	—	0.003	0.007	0.010	0.012	0.017	0.011	0.015	0.020
Aug.	—	—	—	—	Nil	0.004	0.006	0.009	0.013	0.008	0.012	0.017
Sep.	—	—	—	—	—	Nil	0.003	0.005	0.010	0.004	0.008	0.013
Oct.	—	—	—	—	—	—	Nil	0.002	0.007	0.002	0.005	0.010
Nov.	—	—	—	—	—	—	—	Nil	0.005	Nil	0.003	0.008
Dec.	—	—	—	—	—	—	—	—	Nil	Nil	Nil	0.003
2005 Jan.	—	—	—	—	—	—	—	—	—	Nil	Nil	0.008
Feb.	—	—	—	—	—	—	—	—	—	—	0.004	0.005
Mar.	—	—	—	—	—	—	—	—	—	—	—	Nil

Double tax treaties

The following table lists all the territories with which the UK has concluded agreements to avoid international double taxation and also facilitate the exchange of information to prevent tax evasion. These agreements may be of various types which are indicated below by the following letters:

- (C) – comprehensive agreements covering a wide range of areas of possible double taxation of income and capital gains;
- (SA) – agreements limited to shipping and air transport profits;
- (A) – agreements limited to air transport profits only;
- (EIG) – agreements relating to tax on estates, inheritances and gifts;
- (TIE) – tax information exchange agreements relating to the taxation of savings income received by individuals; and
- (EC) – tax information exchange agreements concluded by the EC on behalf of its member states with third countries.

Algeria (A)
Andorra (EC)
Antigua and Barbuda (C)
Argentina (C)
Australia (C)
Austria (C/SS)
Azerbaijan (C)
Bangladesh (C)
Barbados (C/SS)
Belarus (C)[(1)(3)]
Belgium (C/SS)
Belize (C)
Bermuda (SS)
Bolivia (C)
Bosnia-Herzegovina (C/SS)[(2)]
Botswana (C)
Brazil (S/A)
Brunei (C)
Bulgaria (C)
Burma (Myanmar) (C)
Cameroon (A)
Canada (C/SS)
Chile (C)[(3)]
China (C/A)
Croatia (C/SS)[(2)]
Cyprus (C/SS)
Czech Republic (C)
Denmark (C/SS)
Egypt (C)
Estonia (C/SS)[(1)]
Ethiopia (A)
Falkland Islands (C)
Fiji (C)
Finland (C/SS)
France (includes Guadeloupe,
    Guyane, Martinique and
    Réunion (C/EIG/SS)
Gambia (C)
Georgia[(3)]
Germany (C/SS)
Ghana (C)
Gibraltar (SS)
Greece (C/SS)

Grenada (C)
Guernsey (includes Alderney,
    Herm and Lithou) (C/SS/TIE)
Guyana (C)
Hong Kong SAR (S/A)
Hungary (C/SS)
Iceland (C/SS)
India (C/EIG)[(4)]
Indonesia (C)
Iran (A)
Irish Republic (C/EIG/SS)
Isle of Man (C/SS/TIE)
Israel (C/SS)
Italy (C/EIG/SS)
Ivory Coast (Cote d'Ivoire) (C)
Jamaica (C/SS)
Japan (C/SS)
Jersey (C/SS/TIE)
Jordan (C)
Kazakstan (C)
Kenya (C)
Kiribati (C)
Kuwait (C)
Latvia (C)
Lebanon (S/A)
Lesotho (C)
Liechtenstein (SS/EC)
Lithuania (C/SS)
Luxembourg (C/SS)
Macedonia (C/SS)[(2)]
Malawi (C)
Malaysia (C)
Malta (C/SS)
Mauritius (C/SS)
Mexico (C)
Monaco (EC)
Mongolia (C)
Montserrat (C/TIE)
Morocco (C)
Namibia (C)
Netherlands (C/E/I/G/SS)
New Zealand (C/SS)
Nigeria (C)

Norway (C/SS)
Oman (C)
Pakistan (C/EIG)[(4)]
Papua New Guinea (C)
Philippines (C/SS)
Poland (C/SS)
Portugal (C/SS)
Romania (C)
Russian Federation (C)
San Marino (EC)
St. Christopher (St. Kitts) & Nevis (C)
Saudi Arabia (A)
Serbia and Montenegro (C/SS) [(2)]
Sierra Leone (C)
Singapore (C)
Slovak Republic (C/SS)
Slovenia (C/SS)[(2)]
Solomon Islands (C)
South Africa (C/EIG)
South Korea (C/SS)
Spain (C/SS)
Sri Lanka (C)
Sudan (C)
Swaziland (C)
Sweden (C/EIG/SS)
Switzerland (C/EIG/SS/EC)
Taiwan (C)
Tajikistan (C)[(1)]
Thailand (C)
Trinidad and Tobago (C)
Tunisia (C)
Turkey (C/SS)
Tuvalu (C)
Turkmenistan (C)[(1)]
Uganda (C)
Ukraine (C)
USA (C/E/I/G/SS)
Uzbekistan (C/A)
Venezuela (C)
Vietnam (C)
Zaire (S/A)
Zambia (C)
Zimbabwe (C)

Notes

[(1)] The Convention of 31 July 1985 with the former USSR is regarded as continuing in force (see SP 04/01).

[(2)] The Convention of 5 November 1981 with the former Yugoslavia is regarded as continuing in force (see SP 03/04).

[(3)] The following treaties were signed and agreed, but not in force, at the time of publication:

- Belarus (C) (see also footnote[(1)] above);

- Georgia (C) (see also footnote (1) above);

[(4)] The estate, inheritance and gifts agreements with India and Pakistan have not been formally terminated despite the fact that estate duties in those countries were abolished on 15 March 1985 and 29 July 1979 respectively.

[(5)] The reciprocal social security arrangements made with EU member states have all, with the exception of parts of the Orders relating to Germany, been superseded by EC Regulation 1408/71 (as codified and amended).

Foreign exchange rates: general

The Revenue publish annually currency exchange rates for the purposes of converting foreign currencies into sterling.

The currency exchange rates for the US dollar, German deutschmark, Japanese yen and euro for 1990–91 and subsequent years are reproduced below.

Average exchange rates for year to 31 December

Average for year to 31 December	US $	DM	Yen	Euro
1994	1.5318	2.4826	156.4429	
1995	1.5783	2.2603	148.283	
1996	1.5619	2.3506 .	169.593	
1997	1.638	2.8391	198.189	
1998	1.6573	2.9147	216.6834	
1999	1.6181	2.9702	183.969	
2000	1.5163	3.2114	163.378	
2001	1.4401	3.1461	174.8889	
2002	1.5023	N/A	187.8315	1.5906
2003	1.6348	N/A	189.3354	1.4457

Average exchange rates for year to 31 March

Average for year to 31 March	US $	DM	Yen	Euro
1995	1.5553	2.4256	154.3941	
1996	1.5656	2.2375	150.75	
1997	1.5866	2.4642	178.8762	
1998	1.642	2.912	201.5651	
1999	1.6542	2.878	211.499	
2000	1.6114	3.0548	179.386	
2001	1.4793	3.1886	163.482	
2002	1.432	3.1677	179.0169	
2003	1.5466	N/A	188.3036	1.5573
2004	1.6348	N/A	190.9326	1.4400

Foreign exchange rates 2003–04

		Average rates for the year to 31 December 2003 and the year to 31 March 2004			
		Average for the year to 31 December 2003		Average for the year to 31 March 2004	
Country	Unit of currency	Currency units per £1	Sterling value of currency unit £	Currency units per £1	Sterling value of currency unit £
Algeria	Algerian Dinar	125.8034	0.007949	126.6578	0.007895
Argentina	Peso	4.8273	0.20716	4.881	0.20488
Australia	Australian Dollar	2.524	0.396197	2.4488	0.408363
Bahrain	Bahrain Dinar	0.6154	1.624959	0.6376	1.568381
Bangladesh	Taka	95.7319	0.01044584	99.4753	0.010053
Barbados	Barbados Dollar	3.2483	0.307853	3.3697	0.296762
Bolivia	Boliviano	12.5163	0.079896	13.1051	0.076306
Botswana	Pula	8.0287	0.12455317	8.0961	0.123516
Brazil	Real	5.0623	0.19754	4.9999	0.2
Brunei	Brunei Dollar	2.8645	0.34910106	2.9419	0.339916
Burma	Kyat	10.1922	0.09811	10.6399	0.09399
Burundi	Burundi Franc	1739.2108	0.00057497	1802.3	0.0006
Canada	Canadian Dollar	2.2881	0.437044	2.2893	0.436815
Cayman Islands	C.I Dollar	1.3487	0.74145473	1.3987	0.71495
Chile	Chilean Peso	1125.31	0.000889	1102.876	0.000907
China	Renminbi	13.6132	0.07345811	14.0961	0.070942
Colombia	Colombia Peso	4592.52	0.00022	4656.48	0.00021
Congo Dem (Rep) Zaire	Congolese Franc	702.3912	0.00142371	719.4719	0.00138991
Costa Rica	Colon	658.5835	0.00151841	699.2543	0.00143
Cuba	Cuban Peso	34.5385	0.0289532	1/4/03–31/12/03 = 34.8824 1/1/04–31/3/04 = 1.8289	1/4/03–31/12/03 = 0.02866775 1/1/04–31/3/04 = 0.54677675
Cyprus	Cyprus Pound	0.8449	1.18357202	0.8467	1.181056
Czech Republic	Koruna	46.0249	0.02172737	46.464	0.021522
Denmark	Danish Krone	10.7423	0.093090	10.7070	0.093397
Ecuador	Sucre	1.6447	0.60801362	1.7031	0.587165
Egypt	Egyptian £	9.5996	0.10417	10.3236	0.09687
El Salvador	Colon	14.3917	0.06948449	14.9044	0.067094
Ethiopia	Ethiopian Birr	13.9118	0.07188142	14.5257	0.068843
European Union	Euro	1.4457	0.691706	1.4400	0.694444
Fiji Islands	Fiji Dollar	3.0924	0.32337343	3.0813	0.324538
French Cty/Africa	C.F.A. Franc	947.6108	0.00105529	947.8783	0.001055
French Pacific Islands	C.F.P. Franc	169.6251	0.00589535	169.7237	0.005892

2003–04 Foreign exchange rates (cont'd)

| | | Average rates for the year to 31 December 2003 and the year to 31 March 2004 | | | |
| | | Average for the year to 31 December 2003 | | Average for the year to 31 March 2004 | |
Country	Unit of currency	Currency units per £1	Sterling value of currency unit £	Currency units per £1	Sterling value of currency unit £
Gambia	Dalasi	44.6984	0.02237217	48.429	0.020649
Ghana	Ghanaian Cedi	14076	0.000071	14825.84	0.0000133
Grenada/Wind. Isles	East Caribbean Dollar	4.3785	0.228389	4.5399	0.220269
Guyana	Guyanese Dollar	292.9325	0.0034138	303.5003	0.0032949
Honduras	Lempira	28.5611	0.03501266	29.9331	0.033408
Hong Kong	H.K. Dollar	12.7301	0.078554	13.1806	0.075869
Hungary	Forint	367.5425	0.00272077	372.2082	0.002687
Iceland	Icelandic Krona	125.1424	0.007991	125.943	0.00794
India	Indian Rupee	76.1738	0.01313	77.7583	0.01286
Indonesia	I.Rupiah	14025.2	0.0000713	14361.3	0.0000696
Iran	Iranian Rial	13411.2	0.0000745	14059.8	0.0000711
Iraq	Iraq Dinar	0.5082	1.96773	1/4/03–20/2/04 = 0.5234 21/2/04–31/3/04 = 2187.62	1/4/03–20/2/04 = 1.9105846 21/2/04–31/3/04 = 0.0004571
Israel	Shekel	7.4392	0.13442	7.5603	0.13227
Jamaica	Jamaican Dollar	93.5725	0.010687	100.3891	0.009961
Japan	Japanese Yen	189.3354	0.005282	190.9326	0.005237
Jordan	Jordanian Dinar	1.1772	0.8494733	1.2188	0.8204792
Kenya	Kenya Shilling	124.3147	0.008044	128.7432	0.007767
Korea(South)	Won	1962.85	0.00050946	2017.287	0.000496
Kuwait	Kuwaiti Dinar	0.4875	2.05128	0.5031	1.98768
Laos	New Kip	12582.15	0.0000794	13154.55	0.000076
Lebanon	Lebanese Pound	2474.628	0.000404	2566.365	0.00039
Libya	Libyan Dinar	2.0808	0.4806	2.1938	0.4558
Malawi	Malawi Kwacha	157.579	0.00635	171.341	0.00584
Malaysia	Ringgit	6.2175	0.160836	6.4423	0.155224
Malta	Maltese Lira	0.616	1.62338	0.6164	1.62232
Mauritius	Rupee	45.8304	0.02182	46.5149	0.021498
Mexico	Mexican Peso	17.6634	0.05661	18.385	0.05439
Morocco	Dirham	15.6655	0.06383454	15.7817	0.063365
Nepal	Nepalese Ruppe	124.1903	0.00805216	126.7737	0.007888
N'nd Antilles	Antilles Guilder	2.9276	0.34157672	3.036	0.329381
New Zealand	N.Z. Dollar	2.8149	0.3552524	2.7677	0.3613108
Nicaragua	Gold Cordoba	24.7196	0.04045373	25.9672	0.03851

2003–04 Foreign exchange rates (cont'd)

Country	Unit of currency	Average for the year to 31 December 2003		Average for the year to 31 March 2004	
		Currency units per £1	Sterling value of currency unit £	Currency units per £1	Sterling value of currency unit £
Nigeria	Nigerian Naira	215.7939	0.004634	226.7154	0.004411
Norway	N. Krone	11.5624	0.086487	11.9099	0.083964
Oman, Sultanate of	Rial Omani	0.63	1.5873	0.6529	1.5316
Pakistan	Pakistan Rupee	94.4568	0.0106	97.6040	0.0102
Papua New Guinea	Kina	5.764	0.17349063	5.7436	0.174107
Paraguay	Guarani	10568.085	0.0001	10556.6188	0.0001
Peru	New Sol	7.0487	0.1419	7.2490	0.1380
Phillipines	Phillipine Peso	88.727	0.0113	92.8336	0.0108
Poland	Zloty	6.0605	0.16500289	6.2744	0.159378
Qatar	Qatar Riyal	5.9559	0.1679	6.1714	0.1620
Romania	Leu	54460.65	0.0000183	56162.18	0.0000178
Russia	Rouble (market)	50.3037	0.01987925	50.7326	0.019711
Rwanda	Rwanda Franc	870.1093	0.00114928	922.732	0.001084
Saudi Arabia	Saudi Riyal	6.1359	0.1630	6.3578	0.1573
Seychelles	Rupee	9.1568	0.10920846	9.4401	0.105931
Sierra Leone	Leone	3794.318	0.0003	4046.3759	0.00024713
Singapore	Singapore Dollar	2.8507	0.3508	2.9295	0.3414
Solomon Islands	S.I. Dollar	12.3836	0.08075196	12.7742	0.078283
Somali Republic	Shilling	4309.0933	0.00023207	4461.972	0.000224
South Africa	Rand	12.3217	0.081158	12.0949	0.082679
Sri Lanka	Rupee	157.8615	0.0063	164.0631	0.0061
Sudan	Sudanese Dinar	428.0218	0.00233633	443.2834	0.002256
Surinam	Surinam Guilder	4090.3075	0.00024448	3134.437	0.000319
Swaziland	Lilangeni	11.3275	0.08828073	12.0136	0.083239
Sweden	Swedish Krona	13.1934	0.075795	13.1427	0.076088
Switzerland	Swiss Franc	2.1973	0.455104	2.2266	0.449115
Syria	Syrian Pound	77.6399	0.01287998	81.2087	0.012314
Taiwan	New T. Dollar	56.2877	0.0178	57.7063	0.0173
Tanzania	Shilling	1699.27	0.00059	1797.86	0.00056
Thailand	Thai Baht	67.8966	0.01473	68.7556	0.01454
Tonga Islands	Pa'Anga	2.6096	0.38320049	2.84	0.352113
Trinidad & Tobago	Trinidad & Tobago Dollar	9.9007	0.101003	10.2507	0.097554
Tunisia	Dinar	2.104	0.47529	2.1393	0.46744
Turkey	Turkish Lira	2456924.1	0.00000040701	2405776.37	0.000000415
Uganda	New Shilling	3210.6078	0.00031147	3327.7742	0.0003005
United Arab Emirates	U.A.E Dirham	6.0083	0.16643643	6.2256	0.16062709

2003–04 Foreign exchange rates (cont'd)

| | | Average rates for the year to 31 December 2003 and the year to 31 March 2004 | | | |
| | | Average for the year to 31 December 2003 | | Average for the year to 31 March 2004 | |
Country	Unit of currency	Currency units per £1	Sterling value of currency unit £	Currency units per £1	Sterling value of currency unit £
Uruguay	Uruguayan Peso	114.6677	0.00872085	116.9099	0.0085536
U.S.A	U.S. Dollar	1.6348	0.611696	1.6939	0.590354
Venezuela	V.Bolivar	2838.118	0.000352	3629.222	0.000276
Vietnam	Dong	25528.083	0.000039	26564.48	0.000038
Yemen	Rial	292.7023	0.00341644	306.0884	0.003267
Zambia	Zambian Kwacha	7809.26	0.00013	8038.83	0.00012
Zimbabwe	Z. Dollar	1141.414	0.000876	2499.284	0.0004

Table of spot rates on 31 December 2002 and 31 March 2003

| Country | Unit of currency | 31 December 2002 | | 28 March 2003 | |
		Currency units per £1	Sterling value of currency unit (£)	Currency units per £1	Sterling value of currency unit (£)
Australia	Australian Dollar	$A. 2.859	0.3497726	$A. 2.6157	0.3823068
Canada	Canadian Dollar	Can.$. 2.5433	0.3931899	Can.$. 2.3251	0.430089
Denmark	Danish Krone	D. Kr. 11.3954	0.0877547	D. Kr. 10.7573	0.0929601
European Union	Euro	€1.5342	0.6518055	€1.4486	0.6903216
Hong Kong	Hong Kong Dollar	H.K.$. 12.5546	0.079652	H.K.$. 12.3282	0.0811148
Japan	Japanese Yen	Y. 191.047	0.0052343	Y. 187.433	0.0053352
Norway	Norwegian Krone	N. Kr. 11.153	0.0896619	N. Kr. 11.4703	0.0871816
South Africa	Rand	R 13.8138	0.0723913	R. 12.4413	0.0803774
Sweden	Swedish Krone	S Kr. 14.0276	0.071288	S Kr. 13.4023	0.074614
Switzerland	Swiss Franc	SwF 2.226	0.4492362	SwF 2.1362	0.4681209
USA	US Dollar	US$ 1.6099	0.6211565	US$ 1.5807	0.6326311

Finance Acts

Year	Budget		Royal Assent	
1972	21 March	1972	27 July	1972
1973	6 March	1973	25 July	1973
1974	26 March	1974	31 July	1974
1975	12 November	1974	13 March	1975
1975 (No. 2)	15 April	1975	1 August	1975
1976	6 April	1976	29 July	1976
1977	29 March	1977	29 July	1977
1978	11 April	1978	31 July	1978
1979	3 April	1979	4 April	1979
1979 (No. 2)	12 June	1979	26 July	1979
1980	26 March	1980	1 August	1980
1981	10 March	1981	27 July	1981
1982	9 March	1982	30 July	1982
1983	15 March	1983	13 May	1983
1983 (No. 2)	15 March	1983	26 July	1983
1984	13 March	1984	26 July	1984
1985	19 March	1985	25 July	1985
1986	18 March	1986	25 July	1986
1987	17 March	1987	15 May	1987
1987 (No. 2)	17 March	1987	23 July	1987
1988	15 March	1988	29 July	1988
1989	14 March	1989	27 July	1989
1990	20 March	1990	26 July	1990
1991	19 March	1991	26 July	1991
1992	10 March	1992	16 March	1992
1992 (No. 2)	10 March	1992	16 July	1992
1993	16 March	1993	27 July	1993
1994	30 November	1993	3 May	1994
1995	29 November	1994	1 May	1995
1996	28 November	1995	29 April	1996
1997	26 November	1996	19 March	1997
1997 (No. 2)	2 July	1997	31 July	1997
1998	17 March	1998	31 July	1998
1999	9 March	1999	27 July	1999
2000	21 March	2000	28 July	2000
2001	7 March	2001	11 May	2001
2002	17 April	2002	24 July	2002
2003	9 April	2003	10 July	2003
2004	17 March	2004	22 July	2004
2005	16 March	2005	7 April	2005

Recognised stock exchanges

'The Stock Exchange' (strictly known as 'The International Stock Exchange of the United Kingdom and the Republic of Ireland Ltd') is a 'recognised stock exchange'; the stock exchanges of the following countries have also been designated by the Board of Inland Revenue as 'recognised stock exchanges'. Where there is no specific or unified exchange shown there is included any exchange recognised by the laws of that country (ICTA 1988, s. 841; TCGA 1992, s. 288(1)).

Note that the Revenue explained a revised interpretation of 'listed on a recognised stock exchange' in a press release of 28 November 2001. This had the effect of reversing the previous view of securities traded on EU 'junior' markets and NASDAQ Europe (formerly EASDAQ) which are now treated as unlisted (although with transitional provisions in place).

In a Policy Statement dated 27 November 2002 the Revenue announced that it would be taking a more broadly-based approach.

Below is a list of stock exchanges designated as 'recognised stock exchanges' by Order of the Board of Inland Revenue, under ICTA 1988, s. 841(1)(b), with the date of recognition.

The Athens Stock Exchange	14 Jun 1993
The Australian Stock Exchange and any of its stock exchange subsidiaries[1]	22 Sep 1988
The Cayman Islands Stock Exchange	4 Mar 2004
The Colombo Stock Exchange	21 Feb 1972
The Copenhagen Stock Exchange	22 Oct 1970
The Helsinki Stock Exchange	22 Oct 1970
The Johannesburg Stock Exchange	22 Oct 1970
The Korea Stock Exchange	10 Oct 1994
The Kuala Lumpur Stock Exchange	10 Oct 1994
The Mexico Stock Exchange	10 Oct 1994
The New Zealand Stock Exchange	22 Sep 1988
The Rio De Janeiro Stock Exchange	17 Aug 1995
The Sao Paulo Stock Exchange	11 Dec 1995
The Singapore Stock Exchange	30 Jun 1977
The Stockholm Stock Exchange	16 Jul 1985
The Stock Exchange of Thailand	10 Oct 1994

The Swiss Stock Exchange[2]	12 May 1997

Notes
[1] Replaces an Order dated 22 October 1970 recognising any Australian stock exchange which was a prescribed member exchange of the Australian Associated Stock Exchanges.
[2] Formed on the merger of the Zurich, Basle and Geneva exchanges, that were all previously recognised by an Order dated 30 June 1970.

Any stock exchange in the following countries which is a stock exchange within the meaning of the law of the particular country relating to stock exchanges (or as specified below).

Austria	22 Oct 1970
Belgium (including EASDAQ)	22 Oct 1970
Canada – Any stock exchange prescribed for the purpose of the Canadian Income Tax Act	22 Oct 1970
France	22 Oct 1970
Germany	5 Aug 1971
Guernsey	10 Dec 2002
Hong Kong – Any stock exchange which is recognised under s. 2A(1) of the Hong Kong Companies Ordinance	26 Feb 1971
Italy	3 May 1972
Republic of Ireland[1]	22 Oct 1970
Japan	22 Oct 1970
Luxembourg	21 Feb 1972
Netherlands	22 Oct 1970
Norway	22 Oct 1970
Portugal	21 Feb 1972
Spain	5 Aug 1971
USA – Any exchange registered with the Securities and Exchange Commission of the United States as a national securities exchange	22 Oct 1970
USA – the NASDAQ Stock Market as maintained through the facilities of the National Association of Securities Dealers, Inc. and its subsidiaries	10 Mar 1992

Note
[1] On 23 March 1973, the stock exchanges in the Republic of Ireland became part of 'the Stock Exchange'. In December 1995, the Irish Stock Exchange demerged from 'the Stock Exchange'.

Recognised futures exchanges

The following futures exchanges have been designated by the Board of Inland Revenue as 'recognised futures exchanges' (TCGA 1992, s. 288(6))[1]:

Notes
[1] When the Board recognises a futures exchange this is announced in the *London Gazette*.

Date	Exchange
From 6 August 1985	International Petroleum Exchange of London London Metal Exchange London Wool Terminal Market
From 12 December 1985	London Gold Market London Silver Market
From 19 December 1986	Chicago Mercantile Exchange Philadelphia Board of Trade New York Mercantile Exchange
From 24 April 1987	Chicago Board of Trade
From 29 July 1987	Montreal Exchange Mid-America Commodity Exchange
From 15 December 1987	Hong Kong Futures Exchange New York Coffee Sugar and Cocoa Exchange
From 25 August 1988	Commodity Exchange, Inc (COMEX) Citrus Associates of the New York Cotton Exchange Inc New York Cotton Exchange
From 31 October 1988	Sydney Futures Exchange Ltd
From 18 March 1992	OM Stockholm London Commodity Exchange[2] OMLX (formerly OM London)
From 22 March 1992	London International Financial Futures and Options Exchange (LIFFE)[3]

Notes
[2] The following futures exchanges, which are recognised from 6 August 1985, are now part of the London Commodity Exchange: Baltic International Freight Futures Exchange; London Cocoa Terminal Market; London Coffee Terminal Market; London Futures and Options Exchange; London Grain Futures Market; London Meat Futures Market; London Potato Futures Market; London Rubber Market; London Soya Bean Meal Futures Market; London Sugar Terminal Market. The name of the London International Financial Futures Exchange changed to London Commodity Exchange from 1 July 1993.
[3] The London International Financial Futures Exchange and the London Traded Options Market merged on 22 March 1992, forming the London International Financial Futures and Options Exchange (LIFFE).

Recognised clearing systems

The following clearing systems were designated by an Order of the Board of Inland Revenue, dated 9 May 1996 and noted in the *London Gazette* on 23 May 1996, as 'recognised clearing systems' (ICTA 1988, s. 841A, for the purposes of s. 124(2), both of which were repealed with effect for interest paid on or after 1 April 2001):

Country	Clearing system	Effective date
Belgium	Euroclear	26 July 1984
Luxembourg	Cedel	26 July 1984
United Kingdom	Bank of England European Settlements Office First Chicago Clearing Centre	16 August 1993 14 October 1988
United States	The Depository Trust Co	18 July 1995

Note

ICTA 1988, s. 841A is repealed for payments of interest made on or after 1 April 2001 (FA 2000, s. 156 and Sch. 40, Pt. 11(17)).

Recognised investment exchanges

A 'recognised investment exchange' is an investment exchange in relation to which a recognition order made by the Financial Services Authority is in force (*Financial Services and Markets Act* 2000, s. 285ff.). Prior to the *Financial Services and Markets Act* 2000 coming into force, the *Financial Services Act* 1986, s. 37 applied, so that a 'recognised investment exchange' was one which had a recognition order from the Secretary of State. Securities traded on such an exchange are treated in the same way for tax purposes as those traded on 'The Stock Exchange' (strictly known as 'The International Stock Exchange of the United Kingdom and the Republic of Ireland Ltd') (FA 1986, Sch. 18, para. 8; F(No. 2)A 1987, s. 73; ICTA 1988, s. 841(3)).

From 22 March 1992: London International Financial Futures Exchange (Administration and Management) (LIFFE (A & M)).

STAMP TAXES

Rates, penalties and interest

Conveyance or transfer on sale of shares and securities (FA 1999, Sch. 13, para. 3)

Instrument	Rate of tax after 26 October 1986 %
Stock transfer	$1/_2$ [1][2]
Conversion of shares into depositary receipts	$1 1/_2$ [3]
Take overs and mergers	$1/_2$ [1][2]
Purchase by company of own shares	[1][2]
Letters of allotment	$1/_2$

Notes
[1] Because duty at $1/_2$% is equivalent to £5 per £1,000 of consideration and duty is rounded up to the next multiple of £5 (FA 1999, s. 112(1)(b)), duty is effectively £5 per £1,000 (or part of £1,000) of consideration.
[2] Loan capital is generally exempt from transfer on sale duty subject to specific exclusions (designed to prevent exemption applying to quasi-equity securities) (FA 1986, s. 79).
[3] FA 1986, s. 67(3).

Transfers of property stamp duty land tax (SDLT) (consideration paid)

Rates from 17 March 2005

All land in UK

Rate (%)	Residential	Non-residential
Zero	£120,000	£150,000
1	Over £120,000–£250,000	Over £150,000–£250,000
3	Over £250,000–£500,000	Over £250,000–£500,000
4	Over £500,000	Over £500,000

Land in disadvantaged areas

Rate (%)	Residential	Non-residential[1]
Zero	£150,000	£150,000
1	Over £150,000–£250,000	Over £150,000–£250,000
3	Over £250,001–£50,000	Over £250,001–£50,000
4	Over £500,000	Over £500,000

[1] The exemption for non-residential transactions in land situated in a disadvantaged area was abolished for transactions with an effective date after 16 March 2005. Certain contracts entered into before then where the transaction takes place after abolition may continue to benefit from exemption.

Rates from 1 December 2003 to 16 March 2005

All land in UK

Rate (%)	Residential	Non-residential
Zero	£60,000	£150,000
1	Over £60,000–£250,000	Over £150,000–£250,000
3	Over £250,000–£500,000	Over £250,000–£500,000
4	Over £500,000	Over £500,000

Land in disadvantaged areas

Rate (%)	Residential	Non-residential
Zero	£150,000	All
1	Over £150,000–£250,000	
3	Over £250,001–£50,000	
4	Over £500,000	

Note
FA 2003, s. 125 confirms that property that is not land, shares or interests in partnerships is not subject to stamp duty from 1 December 2003.

Conveyance or transfer on sale of other property (e.g. freehold property)

Rates from 9 April 2003 to 30 November 2003

Rate (%)	All property	Disadvantaged areas	
		Residential	Non-residential
Zero	£0–£60,000	£0–£150,000	All
1	Over £60,000–£250,000	Over £150,000–£250,000	
3	Over £250,000–£500,000	Over £250,000–£500,000	
4	Over £500,000	Over £500,000	

Rates prior to 9 April 2003 (FA 1999, Sch.13, para. 4)

		Thresholds		
Instruments executed	**Up to £60,000**	**Over £60,000 up to £250,000**	**Over £250,000 up to £500,000**	**Over £500,000**
On or after 28 March 2000[1]	Nil	1%	3%	4%
On or after 16 March 1999[2]	Nil	1%	2.5%	3.5%

Notes

[1] Transfers executed on or after 28 March 2000 unless in pursuance of a contract made on or before 21 March 2000.

[2] Transfers executed on or after 16 March 1999 unless in pursuance of a contract made on or before 9 March 1999.

Stamp duty at the appropriate rate is charged on the *full* amount of the certified value, not just on any excess over a threshold. There is no duty on transfers listed in the table on p. 152.

Fixed duties (FA 1999, s. 112(2))

In relation to instruments executed on or after 1 October 1999, the amount of fixed stamp duty is £5.

Leases (and agreements for leases) (FA 1999, Sch. 13, para. 11–13)

Rates for instruments executed after 27 March 2000

Term (FA 1999, Sch. 13, para. 12(3))	**Rate %**
Under 7 years or indefinite:	
• rent £5,000 or less	Nil
• over £5,000	1
Over 7 but not over 35 years	2
Over 35 but not over 100 years	12
Over 100 years	24

Notes

[1] Leases for a definite term of less than one year: fixed duty of £5 (FA 1999, Sch. 13, para. 11 with effect from 1 October 1999).

[2] Where a furnished property lease is granted for a premium, this will be subject to stamp duty as set out in the table on p. 147 with the nil rate only applying if the annual rent does not exceed £600 per annum.

[3] An agreement for lease is liable to stamp duty as if it were an actual lease, but if a lease is subsequently granted which is in conformity with the agreement, or which relates to substantially the same property and term of years as the agreement, the duty on the lease is reduced by the duty already paid on the agreement.

Duty on new leases from 17 March 2005

Duty on rent

| Rate (%) | Net present value of rent | |
	Residential	Non-residential
Zero	£0–£120,000	£0–£150,000
1	Over £120,000	Over £150,000

Notes
(1) Duty on premium is the same as for transfers of land (except special rules apply for premium where rent exceeds £600 annually).

Duty on new leases 1 December 2003–16 March 2005

Duty on rent[1]

| Rate (%) | Net present value of rent | |
	Residential	Non-residential
Zero	£0–£60,000	£0–£150,000
1	Over £60,000	Over £150,000

Notes
(1) These rates were introduced by FA 2003, s. 56 and Sch. 5.
(2) Duty on premium is the same as for transfers of land (except special rules apply for premium where rent exceeds £600 annually).

Penalty for late presentation of documents for stamping

Documents executed after 30 September 1999 (SA 1891, s. 15B)

Type of document	Penalties applicable if document presented for stamping more than
Document executed in UK	30 days after execution
Document executed abroad relating to UK land and buildings	30 days after execution (wef Royal assent to FA 2002)
Other document executed abroad	30 days after document first received in UK[1]

Note
(1) Free standing penalty (see table further below) may apply if written information confirming date of receipt in UK is incorrect.

The maximum penalties are:

- £300 or the amount of duty, whichever is less; on documents submitted up to one year late; and
- £300 or the amount of duty, whichever is greater; on documents submitted more than one year late.

Mitigated penalties due on late stamping

The Stamp Office publishes tables (booklet SO10) of mitigated penalty levels that will be applied in straightforward cases.

Cases involving ad valorem duties

Months late	Up to £300	£300–£700	£705–£1,350	£1,355–£2,500	£2,505–£5,000	Over £5,000
Under 3	Nil	£20	£40	£60	£80	£100
Under 6	£20*	£40	£60	£80	£100	£150
Under 9	£40*	£60	£80	£100	£150	£200
Under 12	£60*	£80	£100	£150	£200	£300
Under 15	15% of the duty or £100 if greater					
Under 18	25% of the duty or £150 if greater					See
Under 21	35% of the duty or £200 if greater					below
Under 24	45% of the duty or £250 if greater					

Note
* Or the amount of the duty if that is less.

Cases over one year late involving duty over £5,000 and any case over two years late are considered individually.

Cases involving fixed duties

	Maximum penalty per document	Penalty after mitigation
Up to 12 months late	£5	Nil (100% mitigation)
Over 12 months late	£300	According to circumstances

In all cases above the penalties will not apply if the person responsible for stamping can show a 'reasonable excuse' for the failure to submit the document(s) within the time limit. Interest is due on any unpaid penalty.

Free standing penalties (maximum amount)

- fraud in relation to stamp duty; (£3,000)
- failure to set out true facts, relating to stamp duty liability, in a document; (£3,000)
- failure to stamp document within 30 days of issue of a Notice of Decision on Adjudication; (£300)
- failure to allow inspection of documents; (£300)
- registering or enrolling a chargeable document that is not duly stamped; (£300)
- circulating a blank transfer; (£300)
- issuing an unstamped foreign security. (£300)

Duties abolished since March 1985

Duty	Effective date of abolition
Ad valorem	
• Capital duty	Transactions after 15 March 1988 – documents stamped after 21 March 1988
• Gifts inter vivos	Instruments executed after 18 March 1985, stamped after 25 March 1985
• Life assurance policy duty	Instruments executed after 31 December 1989
• Transfers on divorce etc.	Instruments executed after 25 March 1985
• Unit trust instrument duty	Instruments executed after 15 March 1988, stamped after 21 March 1988
• Variations and appropriations on death	Instruments executed after 25 March 1985
• Transfers of loan capital (subject to specific exclusions) generally (replaced previous provisions excepting certain categories of loan capital)	Instruments executed after 31 July 1986
• Duty on Northern Ireland bank notes etc.	1 January 1992
• Transfers of intellectual property	Instruments executed after 27 March 2000
• Transfers to Registered Social Landlords	Instruments executed after 28 July 2000
• Stamp duty reserve tax on transfers of units or shares in collective investment schemes held in individual pension accounts (IPAs)	Transactions from 1 April 2001
• Transfers of residential land and leases in designated disadvantaged areas (for consideration/premium up to £150,000)[1]	Instruments executed after 29 November 2001. (Exemption of the whole of consideration for non-residential property abolished after 16 March 2005.)
• Transfers of goodwill	Instruments executed after 22 April 2002
• Transfers of debts and other non-marketable securities	Instruments executed after 30 November 2003

Duty	Effective date of abolition
Fixed duties	
• Agreement or contract made or entered into pursuant to the Highways Act. Appointment of a new trustee, and appointment in execution of a power of any property. Covenant. Deed of any kind whatsoever, not liable to other duties. Letter of power of attorney. Procuration. Revocation of any use or trust of any property by any writing, not being a will. Warrant of attorney. Letter of allotment and letter of renunciation. Scrip certificate, scrip.	Instruments executed after 25 March 1985
• Categories within the *Stamp Duty (Exempt Instruments) Regulations* 1987 (SI 1987/516): A. Trust vesting instrument B. Transfer of bequeathed property to legatee C. Transfer of intestate property to person entitled D. Certain appropriations on death E. Transfer to beneficiary of entitlement to residue F. Certain transfers to beneficiaries entitled under settlements G. Certain transfers in consideration of marriage H. Transfers in connection with divorce I. Transfers by liquidator to shareholder J. Grant of easement for no consideration K. Grant of servitude for no consideration L. Conveyance as voluntary disposition for no consideration M. Variations on death	Instruments executed after 30 April 1987
N. Declaration of trust of life policy	Instruments executed after 30 September 1999

Note
FA 2003, s. 125 confirmed that property that is not land, shares or interests in partnerships is not subject to stamp duty from 1 December 2003.

Stamp duty reserve tax

Principal charge (FA 1986, s. 87)

Subject matter of charge	Rate of tax %
Agreements to transfer chargeable securities[1] for money or money's worth	0.5
Renounceable letters of allotment	0.5
Shares converted into depositary receipts	1.5
but transfer of shares or securities on which stamp duty payable	1
Shares put into clearance system	1.5
but transfer of shares or securities on which stamp duty payable	1

Note

[1] Chargeable securities = stocks, shares, loan capital, units under unit trust scheme (FA 1986, s. 99(3)).

Interest on stamp duty and stamp duty reserve tax (SDRT)

In respect of instruments executed on or after 1 October 1999, interest is chargeable on stamp duty that is not paid within 30 days of execution of a stampable document, wherever execution takes place (*Stamp Act* 1891, s. 15A). Interest is payable on repayments of overpaid duty, calculated from the later of 30 days from the date of execution of the instrument, or lodgement with the Stamp Office of the duty repayable (FA 1999, s. 110). Interest is rounded down (if necessary) to the nearest multiple of £5. No interest is payable if that amount is under £25. The applicable interest rate is as prescribed under FA 1989, s. 178.

SDRT carries interest as follows:

- interest is charged on SDRT paid late (TMA 1970, s. 86 via SI 1986/1711, reg. 13);
- repayments of SDRT carry interest from the date that SDRT was paid (FA 1989, s. 178 via SI 1986/1711, reg. 11); and
- similarly, SDRT is repaid with interest if an instrument is duly stamped within six years of the date of the agreement (FA 1986, s. 92).

For interest periods from 1 October 1999 onwards, the rate of interest charged on underpaid or late paid stamp duty and SDRT exceeds that on repayments:

	Rate %	
Period of application	Underpayments	Repayments
From 6 November 2001	6.50	2.50
6 May 2001 to 5 November 2001	7.50	3.50
5 February 2000 to 5 May 2001	8.50	4.00
1 October 1999 to 5 February 2000	7.50	3.00

VALUE ADDED TAX

Rates

Period of application	Standard rate %	Higher rate %
From 1/4/91	17$\frac{1}{2}$	N/A
18/6/79–31/3/91	15	N/A
12/4/76–17/6/79	8	12$\frac{1}{2}$
1/5/75–11/4/76	8	25[1]

Notes

[1] Re petrol, electrical appliances and luxury goods.

[2] Re petrol.

[3] Supplies of fuel and power for domestic, residential and charity non-business use and certain other supplies are charged at five per cent (VATA 1994, Sch. 7A).

[4] Imports of certain works of art, antiques and collectors' items are charged at an effective rate of five per cent from 27 July 1999 (VATA 1994, s. 21(4)–(6) as inserted by FA 1995, s. 22(1) and as amended by FA 1999, s. 12(1)(b)).

[5] The zero rate has applied from 1 April 1973 to date.

Fractions

Fractions are used to determine the amount of VAT at a given rate contained in a tax-inclusive figure.

Example

VAT rate 17$\frac{1}{2}$%

VAT fraction is $17\frac{1}{2}/117\frac{1}{2} = \frac{7}{47}$

Retail price (excluding VAT) £1; VAT at 17$\frac{1}{2}$% = 17$\frac{1}{2}$p.

Retail price (including VAT) £1.17$\frac{1}{2}$; multiply by $\frac{7}{47}$ = 17$\frac{1}{2}$p.

VAT rate %	VAT fraction
5	1/21
2$\frac{1}{2}$	1/41
8	2/27
10	1/11
12$\frac{1}{2}$	1/9
15	3/23
17$\frac{1}{2}$	7/47
25	1/5

Registration limits

(1) Taxable supplies

Past turnover limits

Period of application	Past turnover (£)		Future turnover (£)
	1 year £	Unless turnover for next year will not exceed £	30 days £
From 1/4/05	60,000	58,000	60,000
1/4/04–31/03/05	58,000	56,000	58,000
10/4/03–31/3/04	56,000	54,000	56,000
25/4/02–9/4/03	55,000	53,000	55,000
1/4/01–24/4/02	54,000	52,000	54,000
1/4/00–31/3/01	52,000	50,000	52,000
1/4/99–31/3/00	51,000	49,000	51,000
1/4/98–31/3/99	50,000	48,000	50,000

Future prospects rule: in addition, *future taxable* turnover must be considered. Registration is required if there are reasonable grounds for believing that the value of *taxable* supplies in a period of 30 days (prior to 21 March 1990 this period was one year) will exceed the given limit. This limit is the same as that for the 12 months above, but applies to 30 days from any time.

Notes

Taxable supplies at *both* the zero rate and positive rates are included in the above limits. *All* of a person's taxable supplies are considered, because it is 'persons' not 'businesses' who can or must register.

These limits are *exclusive* of VAT as VAT is not chargeable unless a person is registered or liable to be registered.

Quarter means *calendar* quarter to the end of March, June, September or December.

The limit which applies for a particular past period is that which is in force at the *end* of the period.

There are now two *alternative* tests of the liability to notify Customs of a person's liability to register as a result of making taxable supplies:

(1)   past 12 months turnover limit; and

(2)   future 30 days turnover limit.

The following are *excluded* from the supplies for the purpose of applying the registration limits (VATA 1994, Sch. 1; Notices 700/1 and 700/2).

(1)   value of capital supplies (other than of land)

(2)   any taxable supplies which would not be taxable supplies apart from VATA 1994, s. 7(4), which concerns removal of goods to the UK.

Any supplies made at a previous time when the person was registered are *disregarded* if all necessary information was given to Customs when the earlier registration was cancelled.

If a person took over a business as a 'going concern', he is *deemed* to have made the vendor's supplies for the purposes of registration.

(2) Supplies from other member states

Period of application	Cumulative relevant supplies from 1 January in year to any day in same year £
From 1/1/93	70,000

(VATA 1994, Sch. 2; Notice 700/1).

If certain goods, which are subject to excise duty, are removed to the UK, the person who removes the goods is liable to register in the UK because all such goods must be taxed in the country of destination. There is no de minimis limit.

(3) Acquisitions from other member states

Period of application	Cumulative relevant supplies from 1 January in year to any day in same year £
From 1/4/05	60,000
1/4/04–31/03/05	58,000
10/4/03–31/3/04	56,000
25/4/02–9/4/03	55,000
1/4/01–24/4/02	54,000
1/4/00–31/3/01	52,000
1/4/99–31/3/00	51,000
1/4/98–31/3/99	50,000

Future prospects rule: a person is also liable to register at any time if there are reasonable grounds for believing that the value of his relevant acquisitions in the period of 30 days then beginning will exceed the given limit. This limit is the same as that for the period starting on 1 January above (VATA 1994, Sch. 3; Notice 700/1).

(4) Assets supplied in the UK by overseas persons

From 21 March 2000, any person without an establishment in the UK making or intending to make 'relevant' supplies must VAT register, regardless of the value of those supplies (VATA 1994, Sch. 3A). 'Relevant' supplies are taxable supplies of goods, including capital assets, in the UK where the supplier has recovered UK VAT under the eighth or thirteenth VAT directive. This applies where:

- the supplier (or his predecessor in business) was charged VAT on the purchase of the goods, or on anything incorporated in them, and has either claimed it back or intends to do so; or
- the VAT being claimed back was VAT paid on the import of goods into the UK.

(5) Electronic services

A person can register under VATA 1994, Sch. 3B if he makes or intends to make qualifying supplies, i.e. electronically supplied services to a person who belongs in the UK or another member state and who receives such services otherwise than for business purposes. The

158

person who registers must have neither a business establishment nor a fixed establishment in the UK or in another member state in relation to any supply. Generally the person must also be neither registered nor required to be registered for VAT in the UK or the Isle of Man or, under equivalent legislation, in another member state.

De-registration limits

(1) Taxable supplies

De-registration at any time

A registered person ceases to be liable to be registered if at *any* time Customs are satisfied that the value of his taxable supplies in the period of one year then beginning will not exceed a certain limit. The limits and periods of application are set out below:

Period of application	Future turnover £
From 1/4/05	58,000
1/4/04–31/03/05	56,000
10/4/03–31/3/04	54,000
25/4/02–9/4/03	53,000
1/4/01–24/4/02	52,000
1/4/00–31/3/01	50,000
1/4/99–31/3/00	49,000
1/4/98–31/3/99	48,000

Notes

The value of supplies of capital assets is *excluded* from the supplies for the purpose of applying the de-registration limits.

The de-registration limits *exclude* VAT.

Taxable supplies at both the *zero* rate and positive rates are included in the above limits (VATA 1994, Sch. 1; Notice 700/11).

Since 15 May 1987 the question of de-registration is determined by the above test only, i.e. only *future turnover* is relevant.

(2) Supplies from other member states

Period of application	Past relevant supplies in last year to 31 December £	Future relevant supplies in immediately following year £
From 1/1/93	70,000	70,000

(3) Acquisitions from other member states

Period of application	Past relevant acquisitions in last year to 31 December £	Future relevant acquisitions in immediately following year £
From 1/4/05	60,000	60,000
1/4/04–31/03/05	58,000	58,000
10/4/03–31/3/04	56,000	56,000
25/4/02–9/4/03	55,000	55,000
1/4/01–24/4/02	54,000	54,000
1/4/00–31/3/01	52,000	52,000
1/4/99–31/3/00	51,000	51,000
1/4/98–31/3/99	50,000	50,000

(4) Assets supplied in the UK by overseas persons

If Customs are satisfied that a person registered under VATA 1994, Sch. 3A has ceased to make relevant supplies, Customs can de-register the person from the date on which he so ceased or from an agreed later date. However, Customs must not de-register a person unless they are satisfied that he is not liable to be registered under another provision in VATA 1994.

(5) Electronic services

Customs cancel a person's registration under VATA 1994, Sch. 3B if he notifies them, or they determine, that he ceased to make, or have the intention of to make, qualifying supplies.

Special accounting limits

Cash accounting: admission to the scheme

Period of application	Annual turnover limit[1] £
From 1/4/04	660,000
1/4/01–31/3/04	600,000
1/4/93–31/3/01	350,000
1/10/90–31/3/93	300,000

Note

[1] Includes zero-rated supplies, but excludes any capital assets previously used in the business. Exempt supplies are also excluded.

[2] A person must withdraw from the cash accounting scheme at the end of the prescribed accounting period if the value of his taxable supplies in the one year ending at the end of the prescribed accounting period has exceeded (from 1 April 2004) £825,000 (*Value Added Tax Regulations* 1995 (SI 1995/2518), Pt. VIII; Notice 731).

(3) Outstanding VAT on supplies made and received while using the cash accounting scheme may be brought into account on a cash basis for a further six months after withdrawal from the scheme, but only where withdrawal was voluntary or because the turnover threshold was exceeded.

Annual accounting: admission to the scheme

Period of application	Annual turnover limit[1] £
From 1/4/04	660,000
1/4/01–31/3/04	600,000
9/4/91–31/3/01	300,000

Note
(1) Positive and zero-rated supplies excluding any supplies of capital assets and any exempt supplies.
(2) A person must withdraw from the annual accounting scheme at the end of a prescribed accounting period if the value of his taxable supplies in the one year ending at the end of the prescribed accounting period has exceeded (from 1 April 2004) £825,000 (*Value Added Tax Regulations* 1995 (SI 1995/2518) Pt. VII; Notice 732).
(3) Persons with a taxable turnover of up to (from 10 April 2003) £150,000 may join the annual accounting scheme immediately, i.e. without having to be registered for at least 12 months.

Flat-rate scheme for small businesses: admission to the scheme

Period of application	Annual taxable turnover limit[1] £	Annual total turnover limit[2] £
Returns ending after 9/4/03	150,000	187,500
Returns ending after 25/4/02	100,000	125,000

Note
(1) Zero-rated and positive-rated supplies excluding VAT. Exempt supplies are excluded.
(2) Total of VAT-exclusive turnover and exempt and/or other non-taxable income.
(3) Net VAT liability is calculated by applying a flat-rate percentage to the VAT-inclusive turnover. The flat-rate percentage depends upon the trader sector (Notice 733). However from 1 January 2004, in the first year of VAT registration, the flat-rate percentage can be reduced by one per cent, i.e. if the normal rate is ten per cent, then nine per cent applies.

Zero-rated supplies

(VATA 1994, Sch. 8)

Group	
1.	Food (this includes most food for human and animal consumption - the exceptions are mainly food supplied in the course of catering, confectionary, pet foods and hot take-away food)
2.	Sewerage services and water (except distilled and bottled water) but not if supplied to industry
3.	Books, pamphlets, newspapers, journals, maps, music etc. (but not stationery and posters)
4.	Talking books for the blind and handicapped and wireless sets for the blind
5.	Construction of buildings etc
6.	Protected buildings
7.	International services
8.	Transport
9.	Caravans and houseboats
10.	Gold
11.	Bank notes
12.	Drugs, medicines, aids for the handicapped etc
13.	Imports, exports etc
14.	Tax-free shops (repealed for supplies made after 30 June 1999)
15.	Charities etc
16.	Clothing and footwear

Notes
Except for exported goods and certain transactions in commodities, a supply is generally not zero-rated *unless* it is included in the zero-rated schedule (VATA 1994, Sch. 8). A supply which can be classified as zero-rated overrides exemption. A supply which is not outside the scope of VAT is standard-rated *unless* it falls within one of the categories of exempt or zero-rated or reduced-rate supplies.

Exempt supplies

(VATA 1994, Sch. 9)

Group	
1.	Land
2.	Insurance
3.	Postal services
4.	Betting, gaming and lotteries
5.	Finance

Group	
6.	Education
7.	Health and welfare
8.	Burial and cremation
9.	Subscriptions to trade unions, professional bodies and other public interest bodies
10.	Sport, sports competitions and physical education
11.	Works of art etc.
12.	Fund-raising events by charities and other qualifying bodies
13.	Cultural services etc.
14.	Supplies of goods where input tax cannot be recovered (from 1 March 2000)
15.	Investment gold (from 1 January 2000)

Notes

The descriptions of the zero-rated and exempt groups are for ease of reference only and do not affect the interpretation of the groups (VATA 1994, s. 96(10)). Some suppliers can unilaterally elect to waive exemption of certain land and buildings (VATA 1994, Sch. 10, para. 2–4).

Reduced-rate supplies

(VATA 1994, Sch. 7A)

Group	
1.	Domestic fuel and power
2.	Installation of energy-saving materials
3.	Grant-funded installation of heating equipment or security goods or connection of gas supply.
4.	Women's sanitary products
5.	Children's car seats
6.	Residential conversions
7.	Residential renovations and alterations

Notes

In the March 2005 Budget, the Chancellor announced that from a date to be advised, the five per cent reduced rate of VAT will apply to advice or information connected with or intended to promote the welfare of elderly or disabled people, or children. Such reduced-rating will apply, for example, to child protection videos or expert advice on the welfare of children or the elderly, when supplied by charities working in these areas. The reduced rate will only apply where the goods and services are not otherwise exempt from VAT.

Partial exemption

The partial exemption rules may restrict the amount of deductible input tax (*Value Added Tax Regulations* 1995 (SI 1995/2518), Pt. XIV; Notice 706).

Where input tax cannot be attributed directly to taxable or exempt supplies (residual input tax), the standard method apportions the residual input tax according to the values of taxable and exempt supplies made in a period. In relation to input tax incurred after 17 April 2002, persons must adjust the input tax deductible under the standard method at the end of their tax year if that amount is substantially different from an attribution based on the use of purchases. 'Substantially' means:

* £50,000 or greater; or
* 50% or more of the value of the residual input tax, but not less than £25,000.

Where the residual input tax is less than £50,000 per year, the standard method can be used, unless the person is defined as a group undertaking under the *Companies Act* 1985 and the residual input tax is greater than £25,000 per year.

The de minimis limit for application of partial exemption rules is as follows:

Period	Exempt input tax not exceeding
Tax years beginning after 30/11/94	• £625 per month on average; and • 50% of total input tax for prescribed accounting period
Periods beginning between 1/4/92 and 30/11/94	• £600 per month on average

Capital goods scheme

(*Value Added Tax Regulations* 1995 (SI 1995/2518), Pt. XV; Notice 706/2)

From 1 April 1990 the capital goods scheme affects the acquisition, etc. by a partially exempt person for use in a business of certain items as follows:

Item	Value	Adjustment period
Computers and computer equipment	£50,000 or more	5 years
Land and buildings[1]	£250,000 or more	10 years (5 years where interest had less than 10 years to run on acquisition)

Note
[1] From 3 July 1997, the capital goods scheme affects:

* civil engineering works; and
* the refurbishment or fitting out of a building by the owner.

Where the capital goods scheme applies, any initial deduction of input tax is made in the ordinary way, but must then be reviewed over the adjustment period by reference to the use of the asset concerned.

Revised rules apply to all capital goods scheme adjustments for intervals starting on or after 10 March 1999, to ensure that such adjustments compare the later use of the asset with the actual initial deduction of input VAT, after any other partial exemption adjustments.

Particulars to be shown on a valid VAT invoice

(*Value Added Tax Regulations* 1995 (SI 1995/2518), Pt. III as amended)

VAT invoices generally where supplied to a person who is also in the UK

1.	An identifying number
2.	The time of the supply
3.	The date of issue of the document
4.	The name, address and registration number of the supplier
5.	The name and address of the person to whom the goods or services are supplied
6.	Before 1 January 2004, the type of supply by reference to the following categories: (a) A supply by sale (b) A supply on hire purchase or any similar transaction (c) A supply by loan (d) A supply by way of exchange (e) A supply on hire, lease or rental (f) A supply of goods made from customer's materials (g) A supply by sale on commission (h) A supply on sale or return or similar terms, or (i) Any other type of supply which the commissioners may at any time by notice specify
7.	A description sufficient to identify the goods or services supplied
8.	For each description, the quantity of the goods or the extent of the services, the rate of VAT and the amount payable, excluding VAT, expressed in any currency. Before 1 January 2004, the VAT-exclusive amount had to be expressed in sterling.
9.	The gross total amount payable, excluding VAT
10.	The rate of any cash discount offered
11.	Before 1 January 2004, each rate of VAT chargeable and the amount of VAT chargeable expressed in sterling, at each such rate
12.	The total amount of VAT chargeable, expressed in sterling
13.	From 1 January 2004, the unit price in relation to countable goods and services. However, the unit price may not need to be shown if it is not normally provided in a particular business sector and is not required by the customer

Generally, until 31 December 2004, Customs accepted VAT invoices in the format required before 1 January 2004.

Persons providing VAT invoices for leasing certain motor cars must state on the invoice whether the car is a qualifying vehicle. This enables the lessee to claim the correct proportion of the VAT charged by the lessor.

The requirements for invoices concerning supplies intra-EU member states are in the *Value Added Tax Regulations* 1995 (SI 1995/2518), reg. 14(2).

Retailers' invoices

If the supplier sells directly to the public, he is only required to issue a VAT invoice if the customer requests it. Furthermore, if the supply is for £250 (before 1 January 2004, £100) or less, *including* VAT, a less-detailed VAT invoice can be issued setting out only the following:

1.	The name, address and registration number of the retailer
2.	The time of the supply
3.	A description sufficient to identify the goods or services supplied
4.	The total amount payable including VAT
5.	The rate of VAT in force at the time of the supply

See Customs Notice 700 concerning the special rules for invoices concerning:

- petrol, derv, paraffin, and heating oil;
- credit cards;
- another form of modified VAT invoice for retailers;
- cash and carry wholesalers;
- computer invoicing; and
- calculation of VAT on invoices.

Continuous supplies of services

Certain additional particulars are required to be shown on a VAT invoice for a supply of continuous services, if the supplier chooses to use the advance invoicing facility (*Value Added Tax Regulations* 1995 (SI 1995/2518), reg. 90). Similar provisions apply for advance invoicing in respect of long leases (reg. 85) and in respect of supplies of water, gas, power, heat, refrigeration and ventilation (reg. 86).

Reckonable dates

The reckonable dates for VAT are:

- *interest on overdue tax*: due date for submission of return (usually last day of month following end of return period);
- *interest on tax incorrectly repaid*: seven days after issue of instruction directing payment of amount incorrectly repaid.

Assessments of interest made after 30 September 1993 are restricted to the last three years (VATA 1994, s. 74(3)).

From 7 September 1994, Customs normally do not assess interest if it does not represent 'commercial restitution'.

From 1 February 1995, Customs normally do not assess interest on voluntary disclosures notified to Customs when the net underdeclaration is £2,000 or less. Customs' policy was already not to assess interest where a current-period adjustment is made.

From 6 July 1998, interest rates are varied (usually from the sixth day of a month) in accordance with a formula based on the average base lending rates of the main clearing banks (*Air Passenger Duty and Other Indirect Taxes (Interest Rate) Regulations* 1998 (SI 1998/1461)).

Civil penalties, surcharge and interest

See above for reckonable dates.

Provision	Current civil penalty etc.	
• VAT evasion conduct involving dishonesty[1]	Amount of VAT evaded or sought to be evaded, subject to mitigation (up to 100%)	
• Incorrect certificates as to zero-rating and reduced-rate certificates re fuel and power etc.	VAT chargeable if certificate had been correct minus any VAT actually charged.	
• Misdeclaration or neglect resulting in understatements or overclaims[1][2]	15% of the VAT which would have been lost if the inaccuracy had not been discovered	
• Repeated misdeclarations resulting in understatements or overclaims[1][3]	15% of the VAT which would have been lost if the inaccuracy had not been discovered	
• Failure to notify liability for registration or change in nature of supplies by person exempted from registration[1][4]	**Period of failure**	**Percentage of relevant VAT**
	9 months or less	5%
	Over 9, but not over 18 months	10%
	Over 18 months	15%

Provision	Current civil penalty etc.
	(Minimum penalty £50) However, the relevant VAT is only calculated from 1 January 1996 rather than any earlier date if the liability to register followed a transfer of a business as a going concern.
• Default interest (VATA 1994, s. 74)	For assessments calculated after 16 March 1993[5] interest does not commence from more than three years prior to the assessment date. However, interest continued to be charged until the related VAT is paid[6]

From 6/9/04	7.5%
6/12/03–5/9/04	6.5%
6/9/03–5/12/03	5.5%
6/11/01–5/9/03	6.5%
6/5/01–5/11/01	7.5%
6/2/2000–5/5/01	8.5%
6/3/99–5/2/2000	7.5%
6/1/99–5/3/99	8.5%
6/7/98–5/1/99	9.5%
6/2/96–5/7/98	6.25%
6/3/95–5/2/96	7%
6/10/94–5/3/95	6.25%
6/1/94–5/10/94	5.5%

• Default surcharge	1st default in surcharge period	2%
	2nd	5%
	3rd	10%
	4th or later	15%

In the case of defaults occurring after 31 March 1992 but before 1 April 1993 the maximum surcharge rate was 20%; before 1 October 1993, a surcharge liability notice could be issued after a second default and the rate was 5% for a first default in a surcharge period, 10% for a second default, 15% for a third or later default (£30 minimum. From 1 October 1993, if the taxpayer's return is late but no VAT is due, the surcharge is nil.)

Provision	Current civil penalty etc.
	Customs generally only issue a surcharge assessment at the 2% or 5% rates for an assessment of at least £400 (£200 for returns where the due date was before 30 December 2001).
	A default surcharge can arise for persons who make monthly payments on account for return periods ending after 31 May 1996.
	In relation to a first default by a firm with an annual turnover of up to £150,000, Customs may write to offer help and advice. However, a subsequent default generally results in the issue of a surcharge liability notice.
• Failure to comply with tribunal direction or summons	Up to £1,000
• Unauthorised issue of VAT invoice[1]	15% (30%: pre-1 November 1995) of the 'VAT' shown or amount attributable to VAT (minimum penalty £50)
• Breach of walking possession agreement	50% of the VAT due or amount recoverable
• Breach of regulatory provision (Note: such a penalty cannot be imposed without a prior written warning (VATA 1994, s. 76(2)).	• Failure to preserve records: £500 • Submission of return or payment is late

Number of relevant failures in 2 years before the failure	Greater of:
0	£5 or 1/6 of 1% of VAT due
1	£10 or 1/3 of 1% of VAT due
2 or more	£15 or 1/2 of 1% of VAT due
• Other breaches	

Provision	Current civil penalty etc.	
	Number of relevant failures in 2 years before the failure	**Prescribed daily rate**
	0 1 2 or more	£5 £10 £15
	Penalty: the number of days of failure (100 maximum) multiplied by above prescribed daily rate (minimum penalty £50)	
● Failure to submit EC sales statements[8]	1st default including that to which the default notice relates 2nd 3rd	£50 per day £10 per day £15 per day
	(Maximum: 100 days – minimum: £50)	
● Inaccurate EC sales statements[8]	£100 for any material inaccuracy on a statement submitted within two years of a penalty notice (itself issued after a second materially inaccurate statement)	
● Failure to notify acquisition of excise duty goods or new means of transport[1][4]	**Period of failure**	**Percentage of relevant VAT**
	3 months or less	5%
	Over 3 months but not over 6 months	10%
	Over 6 months	15%
● Failure to comply with requirements of scheme for investment gold[1]	17.5% of the value of the transaction concerned with effect from the passing of FA 2000	
● Evasion of VAT due on imports	Amount of import VAT evaded after 26 November 2003	
● Contravention of Customs rules relating to exports after 22 December 2003	Penalty of at least £250, but no more than £2,500	

Provision	Current civil penalty etc.
• Failure for VAT periods starting after 31 July 2004 by certain persons to disclose to Customs within the 30-day time-limit the use of a designated (listed) avoidance scheme or a notifiable (hallmarked) scheme that is not a designated scheme (Notice 700/8).	Penalty of 15% of VAT saving in relation to a designated scheme or £5,000 in relation to a notifiable scheme that is not a designated scheme

Notes

[1] Mitigation may be available.

[2] For VAT prescribed accounting periods beginning after 30 November 1993 (although Customs normally applied the rules from 16 March 1993 (Customs News Release 32/93)) a penalty may be assessed if a return understates a person's liability by an amount which is at least the lower of:

- £1m; and
- 30% of the sum of output tax and input tax, the 'gross amount of tax'.

  If a misdeclaration occurs as a result of the failure to draw the attention of Customs to an understated assessment, the reference above to the 'gross amount of tax' should be changed to the 'true amount of tax'.

[3] Repeated misdeclaration penalty may be assessed if:

- there are three or more misdeclared returns within 12 accounting periods;
- the misdeclaration in each period equals or exceeds the lesser of 10% of the 'gross amount of tax' (see (2)) and £500,000;
- Customs have issued a penalty liability notice; and
- At least two further misdeclarations occur during the eight periods completed following the issue of a penalty liability notice. This includes the period in which the notice is issued.

  The above conditions apply to VAT prescribed accounting periods beginning after 30 November 1993, although Customs normally applied the rules from 16 March 1993 (Customs News Release 32/93).

[4] The rates given relate to original assessments made on or after 1 January 1995.

[5] Officially the capping of interest applies to interest on any assessments calculated on or after 1 October 1993, however Customs normally applied the new rules from 16 March 1993 when they were announced (Customs News Release 32/93).

[6] Customs generally do not charge interest where it does not represent commercial restitution (Customs News Release 34/94).

[7] Intrastats (supplementary statistical declarations) – criminal offences:

- failure to submit declaration or to provide requested information – fine up to £2,500 (level 4 on the standard scale);
- a trader who knowingly or recklessly makes a false return, or falsifies a return, is:

  (a) on summary conviction, liable to a fine of up to £2,500 (level 4 on the standard scale) and/or three months imprisonment;

  (b) on indictment, liable to an unlimited fine and/or imprisonment up to two years.

[8] With effect from 27 July 1999 there is a two-year time-limit for assessing penalties relating to EC sales statements.

Interest on overpaid VAT

Interest on overpaid VAT arises under VATA 1994, s. 78 in certain cases of official error. Such interest is not free of income or corporation tax.

Period of application	Interest rate %
From 6/9/04	4
6/12/03–5/9/04	3
6/9/03–5/12/03	2
6/11/01–5/9/03	3
6/5/01–5/11/01	4
6/2/00–5/5/01	5
6/3/99–5/2/00	4
6/1/99–5/3/99	5
1/4/97–5/1/99	6
6/2/93–31/3/97	8

Flat-rate scheme for farmers

(VATA 1994, s. 54)

Period of application	Flate rate addition %
From 1/1/93	4

'Blocked' input tax

Any input tax charged on the following items is' blocked', i.e. non-recoverable:

- motor cars, other than certain motor cars acquired by certain persons but after 31 July 1995 (1) any person can recover input tax on motor cars used exclusively for business and (2) only 50 per cent of VAT on car leasing charges is recoverable if lessee makes any private use of the car and if lessor recovered the VAT on buying the car;

- entertainment, except of employees;

- in the case of claims by builders, articles of a kind not ordinarily installed by builders as fixtures in new houses;

- goods supplied under the second-hand scheme;

- goods imported for private purposes;

- non-business element of supplies to be used only partly for business purposes. This may contravene European law where the supplies are of goods: strictly the input tax is deductible, but output tax is due on non-business use. VAT on supplies not intended for business use does not rank as input tax, so cannot be recovered;

- goods and services acquired by a tour operator for re-supply as a designated travel service; and

- domestic accommodation for directors and their families to the extent of domestic purpose use.

In addition, 'exempt input tax' is not recoverable. From 10 March 1999, the partial exemption simplification rule that allowed some businesses to claim back all their input tax, providing that their exempt input tax is only incurred in relation to certain exempt supplies, has been abolished.

VAT on private fuel (scale charges)

Notice 700/64 explains Customs' views on scale charges.

From 1 May 2005

For prescribed accounting periods *beginning* after 30 April 2005, the following table applies to assess output tax due on fuel used by cars for private journeys if it was provided at below cost from business resources. There is no high business mileage discount.

		12 months £	VAT due per car £	3 months £	VAT due per car £	1 month £	VAT due per car £
Diesel *Cylinder capacity*:	2,000cc or less	945.00	140.74	236.00	35.15	78.00	11.62
	over 2,000cc	1,200.00	178.72	300.00	44.68	100.00	14.89
Petrol *Cylinder capacity*:	1,400cc or less	985.00	146.70	246.00	36.64	82.00	12.21
	over 1,400cc up to 2,000cc	1,245.00	185.43	311.00	46.32	103.00	15.34
	over 2,000cc	1,830.00	272.55	457.00	68.06	152.00	22.64

From 1 May 2004 – 30 April 2005

For prescribed accounting periods *beginning* after 30 April 2004, but before 1 May 2005, the following table applies to assess output tax due on fuel used by cars for private journeys if it was provided at below cost from business resources. There is no high business mileage discount.

	12 months £	VAT due per car £	3 months £	VAT due per car £	1 month £	VAT due per car £
Diesel						
Cylinder capacity: 2,000cc or less	865.00	128.82	216.00	32.17	72.00	10.72
over 2,000cc	1,095.00	163.08	273.00	40.65	91.00	13.55
Petrol						
Cylinder capacity: 1,400cc or less	930.00	138.51	232.00	34.55	77.00	11.46
over 1,400cc up to 2,000cc	1,175.00	175.00	293.00	43.63	97.00	14.44
over 2,000cc	1,730.00	257.65	432.00	64.34	144.00	21.44

VAT publications having legal force

The VAT publications that have legal force are listed in Notice 747.

VAT registration numbers: county code prefixes

Member state	Country code
Austria	AT
Belgium	BE
Cyprus[1]	CY
Czech Republic[1]	CZ
Denmark	DK
Estonia[1]	EE
Finland	FI
France	FR
Germany	DE
Greece	EL
Hungary[1]	HU
Ireland	IE
Italy	IT
Latvia[1]	LV
Lithuania[1]	LT
Luxembourg	LU
Malta[1]	MT
Netherlands	NL
Poland[1]	PL
Portugal	PT
Slovakia[1]	SK
Slovenia[1]	SI

174

Member state	Country code
Spain	ES
Sweden	SE
United Kingdom	GB

(1) This country joined the European Union on 1 May 2004.
(2) On 1 January 2007 Bulgaria and Romania may join the European Union. Turkey may join later.

Customs e-mail address and web site

Customs e-mail address

Generally, Customs accept enquiries by e-mail provided that the VAT registration number is quoted. The e-mail address for each regional office is below:

Scotland

enquiries.sco@hmrc.gsi.gov.uk

Northern Ireland

enquiries.ni@hmrc.gsi.gov.uk

Yorkshire, Humber and the North East

enquiries.yhne@hmrc.gsi.gov.uk

North West England

enquiries.nw@hmrc.gsi.gov.uk

East Midlands

enquiries.em@hmrc.gsi.gov.uk

West Midlands

enquiries.wm@hmrc.gsi.gov.uk

Wales

enquiries.wales@hmrc.gsi.gov.uk

Eastern England

enquiries.estn@hmrc.gsi.gov.uk

London

enquiries.lon@hmrc.gsi.gov.uk

South East England

enquiries.se@hmrc.gsi.gov.uk

South West England

enquiries.sw@hmrc.gsi.gov.uk

South East Central England

enquiries.sec@hmrc.gsi.gov.uk

Customs web site

Customs web site is www.hmrc.gov.uk

National Advice Service (NAS)

Customs National Advice Service replaced the local business advice centres from 2 April 2001 and generally is available between the hours of 8am and 8pm on **0845 010 9000** (+44 208 929 0152 for international callers) Monday to Friday. The line tends to be less busy between 2pm and 4pm and between 5.30pm and 8pm.

VAT and Duties Tribunal

15/19 Bedford Avenue, London WC1B 3AS. Tel: (020) 7612 9700 (web site www.financeandtaxtribunals.gov.uk).

INSURANCE PREMIUM TAX

Imposed on certain insurance premiums where the risk is located in the UK (FA 1994, Pt. III; Notice IPT 1).

Rate

Period of application	Standard rate %	Higher rate %
From 1 July 1999	5	17.5
1 April 1997 to 30 June 1999	4	17.5
1 October 1994 to 31 March 1997	2.5	n/a

Note
[1] From 1 August 1998, the higher rate applies to all travel insurance.

Interest payable on certain assessments

Since 6 February 1996, interest on insurance premium tax is charged at the same rate as under VATA 1994, s. 74.

LANDFILL TAX

Landfill tax was introduced on 1 October 1996 and is collected from landfill site operators (FA 1996, Pt. III; Notices LFT 1 and 2).

Exemption applies to mining and quarrying waste, dredging waste, pet cemeteries and waste from the reclamation of contaminated land.

From 1 October 1999, exemption applies to inert waste used in restoring licensed landfill sites, including the progressive backfilling of active mineral workings.

Rates

Type of waste	Rate (per tonne) £
Inactive waste	2
Active waste:	
1 April 2005 to 31 March 2006	18
1 April 2004 to 31 March 2005	15
1 April 2003 to 31 March 2004	14
1 April 2002 to 31 March 2003	13
1 April 2001 to 31 March 2002	12
1 April 2000 to 31 March 2001	11
1 April 1999 to 31 March 2000	10
1 October 1996 to 31 March 1999	7

The lower rate of tax, which applies to land filled with inactive or inert wastes listed in the *Landfill Tax (Qualifying Material) Order* 1996 (SI 1996/1528), is £2.00 per tonne.

Interest payable on underdeclared landfill tax (FA 1996, Sch. 5, para. 26)

Since 1 April 1997, interest on landfill tax is charged at the same rate as under VATA 1994, s. 74.

Environmental trusts

Site operators making payments to environmental trusts set up for approved environmental purposes can claim a tax credit up to 90 per cent of their contribution – subject to a maximum of 20 per cent of their landfill tax bill in a 12-month period. From 1 August 1999, operators using the scheme have up to an additional month every quarter to claim tax credits. On 15 October 1996, Customs approved an independent body, ENTRUST, as the regulator of environmental trusts. It is responsible for enrolling environmental bodies, maintaining their operation and ensuring that all expenditure complies with the landfill tax requirements.

Credit for landfill site operators

The maximum credit that landfill site operators may claim against their annual landfill tax liability, for contributions made to bodies with objects concerned with the environment, enrolled under the Landfill Tax Credit Scheme, falls to 6 per cent from 6.8 per cent from the start of the landfill tax contribution year on 1 April 2005.

AGGREGATES LEVY

Aggregates levy seeks to incorporate the environmental costs imposed by aggregates extraction into the price of virgin aggregate, and to encourage the use of alternative materials such as wastes from construction and demolition (Notices AGL 1 and 2).

Rate

Period of application	Rate (per tonne) £
From 1 April 2002	1.60

There is no registration threshold for aggregates levy. Any person who commercially exploits aggregate in the UK after 31 March 2002 may be liable to register with Customs and account for aggregates levy (FA 2001, Sch. 4 and the *Aggregates Levy (Registration and Miscellaneous Provisions) Regulations* 2001 (SI 2001/4027), reg. 2).

Generally, 'aggregate' means any rock, gravel or sand together with any other substances which are for the time being incorporated in or naturally occurring with it.

'Commercially exploited' generally means in the course or furtherance of a business the earliest of (FA 2001, s. 16):

- removal from:
    - the originating site;
    - a connected site that is registered under the same name as the originating site; or
    - a site where it had been intended to apply an exempt process to it, but this process was not applied;
- agreement to supply to another person;
- use for construction purchases; and
- mixing with any material or substance other than water, except in permitted circumstances.

Interest payable on underdeclared aggregates levy (FA 2001, Sch. 5, para. 5ff.)

Since 1 April 2002, interest on aggregates levy is charged at the same rate as under VATA 1994, s. 74.

INDEX

References are to page numbers.

184

185